American Burke

AMERICAN POLITICAL THOUGHT
Wilson Carey McWilliams and Lance Banning
Founding Editors

American Burke

THE UNCOMMON LIBERALISM OF
DANIEL PATRICK MOYNIHAN

Greg Weiner

 University Press of Kansas

Published by the University Press of Kansas (Lawrence, Kansas 66046),
which was organized by the Kansas Board of Regents and is operated and
funded by Emporia State University, Fort Hays State University, Kansas
State University, Pittsburg State University, the University of Kansas, and
Wichita State University

Library of Congress Cataloging-in-Publication Data

Weiner, Greg.
American Burke : the uncommon liberalism of Daniel Patrick Moynihan /
Greg Weiner.
    pages cm — (American political thought)
Includes bibliographical references and index.
ISBN 978-0-7006-2096-8 (cloth : acid-free paper)
ISBN 978-0-7006-2349-5 (pbk. : acid-free paper)
ISBN 978-0-7006-2097-5 (ebook)
1. Moynihan, Daniel P. (Daniel Patrick), 1927–2003—Political and social
views. 2. Liberalism—United States. 3. United States—Politics and
government—Philosophy. 4. United States—Social policy—Philosophy.
5. Burke, Edmund, 1729–1797—Political and social views. 6. Legislators—
United States—Biography. 7. Statesmen—United States—Biography. 8.
Scholars—United States—Biography. 9. United States. Congress.
Senate—Biography. I. Title.
e840.8.m68w34 2015
973.92092—dc23

                              2014040566

British Library Cataloguing-in-Publication Data is available.

Printed in the United States of America

For George W. Carey
Requiescat in pace

There is only one political poem of the twentieth century I consider worth remembering, and that is Yeats's "Parnell."

> *Parnell came down the road, he said to a cheering man:*
> *"Ireland shall get her freedom and you still break stone."*

This is the knowledge life gives us, and it is indispensable to politics. And yet how alien to it.

DANIEL PATRICK MOYNIHAN, *COPING*, 1973

The lively sense that liberals have of the possibility of progress is matched by a conservative sense of the possibility of decline. Both concerns need attending.

MOYNIHAN, *COUNTING OUR BLESSINGS*, 1980

Democrats . . . have known good times and bad. Sometimes we have merely endured. But more often, we have embodied a great idea, which is that an elected government can be the instrument of the common purpose of a free people; that government can embrace great causes; and do great things.

MOYNIHAN, *GRIDIRON CLUB*, 1981

Contents

Preface and Acknowledgments

I cannot say I knew Pat Moynihan. I met him; as an aide for several years to one of his closest friends in the US Senate, Bob Kerrey of Nebraska, I was around him occasionally, but only that. My most vivid memory is watching him walk away one night from an anteroom off the minority leader's office on the Senate side of the Capitol. Kerrey had commandeered it to rehearse a presentation his staff had put together on his Social Security reform proposal, a combination of individual accounts and benefit adjustments, a cause in which Moynihan would soon join him. This was before PowerPoint became such a craze, or crutch, that speakers grew incapable of public utterances without it, and it seemed innovative that we were using some form of technology—precisely what that was escapes me now—to present the plan visually. What I do recall is that, for some reason, it included the dancing baby that was the early Internet rage of the mid-1990s, I think to illustrate Kerrey's proposal for endowing every child with a retirement account at birth. Moynihan happened to walk by; Kerrey nabbed him and showed the presentation. Afterward, there was Moynihan, his six-foot-five frame jaunting away, remarking amiably in something just above a mutter, "I'll be goddamned!"

So I did not know him. But I admired him, and it is best to put forth at the outset that this is an admiring book. I hope it is not a fawning one, and the intent is for it to be as objectively exegetical as possible. I have endeavored for the most part neither to object nor to endorse but rather to explain. I trust the reader has picked up this book out of interest in Moynihan's views, not mine, and though I have assumed a perspective on the import and orientation of his thought—and that I do present here—the objective is to allow Moynihan to speak for himself.

The perspective is twofold. First, I will argue that Moynihan was a liberal—I use the term here and throughout in its conversational reference to a politics that believes in a robust ameliorative role for govern-ment—of a type no longer present in American political conversation, what I have chosen to call a "Burkean liberal." It bears emphasizing now, though I repeat the qualification several times in the main body of the text as well, that my claim is not that Burke influenced Moynihan, al-though there are indications that, at least around the margins, he did; explicit references to Burke appear at least two dozen times in Moyni-han's hand in my several hundred pages of notes on his writings, which surely are not comprehensive.

Second, I will contend that American politics is impoverished for the loss of Burkean liberalism and would be enriched by its reclamation, re-gardless of whether one agrees with its tenets. Consequently, in the con-cluding chapter—which, it is vital to emphasize, consists largely of my own ideas, inflected by Moynihan but not attributable to him—I will look beyond Moynihan, drawing on his thought to explore what the ele-ments of a contemporary Burkean liberalism might be. The idea is not that Moynihan's thought contains the elements of a consistent Burkean liberalism free of nuance but rather that it can inspire them. Therefore, I have stated as strong and clear a case for that concept as I can in the closing chapter.

The idea of Burkean liberalism uniting the poles of promise (aspira-tions for government) and prudence (awareness of its limits) may seem contradictory. I contend it is not. Burke is available to liberals of a cer-tain cast, although I shall also argue that Burkean liberals and Burkean conservatives—which is to say Burkeans simply—have more in com-mon with each other than with other partisans who travel under the same labels they do. I contrast Burkean liberals, in the conclusion, with Progressives and Burkean conservatives with Tea Party populists. In any case, the noun seems less important than the modifier; put otherwise, the argument favors neither liberalism nor conservatism as those terms are contemporarily used. Instead, the assertion is that Burkeanism can accommodate a wider range of views than is commonly supposed. My teacher George W. Carey was once asked whether he considered himself a "conservative." Remarking that the word had been drained of meaning in contemporary discourse, he thought for a moment and replied that he considered himself a "Burkean." One could be called worse.

Titles naturally simplify. To call Moynihan an American Burke is to make a simple claim about two immensely complex figures whose most common trait is their defiance of easy labels. The claim is neither that Moynihan was a conservative nor that Burke was a liberal. Neither is true; as the subtitle indicates, Moynihan's liberalism was his own, but he was a liberal through and through. Still, the compatibilities between Burke and Moynihan are striking. There is, of course, the bare biographical fact that both grew from commonplace Irish roots to the heights of statesmanship. But the commonalities run far deeper. Both stood at the intersection of thought and action, scholarship and statesmanship. Each made his name as an advocate for the disadvantaged and oppressed of his day: Burke for the Catholics of Ireland, the colonists of America, the oppressed of India; Moynihan for the dependent poor in America and the imprisoned millions of the Soviet empire. Both made lonely but stirring rhetorical stands against the totalitarianism of their times: Burke against the French Revolution, Moynihan against Leninist tyranny. Both were conserving reformers who valued traditional systems of authority, most primarily the family and, in the phrase of Burke's to which Moynihan most often recurred, the "little platoons" of society—what for Burke were social classes and for Moynihan were ethnic groupings. Each interpreted politics in terms of the observable and concrete rather than the metaphysical and abstract, defended legislative government against executive encroachment, devoted himself to political party—and more.

There are, of course, differences. Recent scholarship has alternately emphasized Burke's resistance to statist solutions to poverty (Yuval Levin) and his sympathy with the emerging class of industrial poor (David Bromwich). In either event, it is difficult to imagine Burke as a New Dealer, as Moynihan clearly was, although certainly it is difficult to imagine anyone in the 1770s as a New Dealer. Nor can one imagine

Moynihan as an apologist for aristocracy. So the title *American Burke* is not intended to affiliate Moynihan wholly with Burke or Burke with Moynihan. Each figure is too complicated for a simple alignment. It is, however, intended to emphasize an intriguing harmony of purpose, method, and style. It is also intended to do honor, as I hope it does, to both.

This project stands a considerable distance in time but not, I contend, in topic from the subject of my last book, James Madison. Both Moynihan and Madison were public men whose thought was indelibly shaped by the practice of politics. Both were systematic thinkers whose systems must be collected and woven together from strands strewn across multiple writings. Both were devoted empiricists bounded by circumstance. That is not to say Moynihan was a Madisonian. In certain respects, he was. Certainly, he was a constitutionalist devoted to the separation of powers. In other respects, however, the affinity is less clear. His concept of the public sphere was probably more expansive than Madison's, for example. But both men stood squarely in the tradition of American political thought, at that unique intersection of theory and practice that has consistently shaped our unfolding constitutional tradition.

This project is not an intellectual biography. It is a précis and analysis of Moynihan's political thought and action. Consequently, I have assessed only those writings and events that seem to me to contribute to an understanding of his underlying ideas on the nature, purposes, and limits of politics. I do not cover every significant event in his career. Some omissions may seem strange. I deal, for instance, with the Zionism-as-racism controversy only tangentially in chapter 3's discussion of Moynihan's tenure at the United Nations, using it instead in chapter 1 as an illustration of his insistence on the integrity of language. Moynihan's "benign neglect" memo appears only briefly because, for all the misapprehension of it, it amounted to tactical advice, not theoretical insight. His service in India is largely passed over; many of his Senate accomplishments do not receive attention; and this book takes no interest in psychoanalytic debates about various features of Moynihan's personality, from whether he drank too much (George F. Will, *Newsweek*, December 7, 1987: "Find out what Moynihan drinks and send a case of the stuff to the other 99 senators") to whether his father's desertion influenced his thinking on the family. For those interested in a comprehensive biography that treats these issues and events while taking Moynihan's ideas seriously, none is better than Godfrey Hodgson's *The Gentleman from New York*.[1] But that is not the project I have undertaken here.

Moreover, as an exercise in political theory rather than history, the presentation is not always chronological. At times it is, and the evolution of Moynihan's ideas on some issues will unfold in narrative form. At others, though, it treats his ideas as the generally consistent whole I believe them to be and hence presents them without regard to chronology. The reader may, of course, trace the dates and contexts of these sources in the notes. Where there is some particular relevance, I have supplied them in the main body of the text. Where I have not, it is because I am endeavoring to interweave disparate strands of what I assert to be a coherent system of thought. But the reader should not necessarily infer from the placement of quotations near each other or near events that they were contemporaneous. In chapter 2, for example, I quote Moynihan's criticisms of the War on Poverty as the War on Poverty unfolds even though he did not, for political reasons, write of them until after he left the Johnson administration.

This study is the product of an extensive review of primary sources. Commentary on Moynihan the man and politician abounds; secondary literature on his political *thought* is scarce, nearly to the point of nonexistence. The primary sources on which I have relied include Moynihan's nineteen books and his hundreds, if not thousands, of speeches, essays, articles, press statements, and more. (I regret that, being new to archival research, I did not record box numbers for items from the Library of Congress, but virtually the whole of the sources I have consulted can be located chronologically in either the press or speech files.) In almost all cases, I have utilized his public writings and utterances—that is, not private correspondence or memoranda. The choice is to treat Moynihan as a public man whose thought was adapted to the political arena. I do not doubt he accommodated the fullness of his private thoughts to the facts of the public realm (though I suspect he did this less than many of his contemporaries), but so did Publius, and this is precisely what makes Moynihan's ideas and American political theory more generally so interesting and applicable. By considering Moynihan in this way, we are also able to encompass a range of scholarly writings that do something scholarly writings no longer do: generalize. This methodological choice also spares the writer the inescapably arbitrary chore of attempting to deduce what Moynihan "really meant" versus what he said for political reasons. It is the public, political man we shall encounter in the pages ahead.

That man is recorded in more than 3,000 boxes of material at the Library of Congress to which Elizabeth B. Moynihan, his widow, kindly gave me access, just as she allowed me access to her own recollections and insights. I am profoundly indebted to her and hope she recognizes the thinker who appears in this book. Kerrey, a close friend of Moynihan's and a mentor beyond compare to me, was an early facilitator of the project, read early drafts, and was a patient adviser when it ran into shoals. Fred Woodward is a writer's and reader's publisher, an enduring source of both candor and encouragement, and a credit to the land of Crockett, even though the historical record will indicate that Crockett left there for a godlier place.

Daniel J. Mahoney of Assumption College, whom I am honored to call a colleague even though I would hardly consider myself his peer, was instrumental at every stage, from the conception of this book over a conversation in my office to editing every draft of every chapter. Bernard J. Dobski was, in this as in all other matters, unfailing in his encouragement and support, as were my other departmental colleagues, Geoffrey Vaughan and Jeremy Geddert. My Philosophy Department colleague Daniel Maher provided invaluable and detailed feedback on the entire manuscript—this while engaged with the rather more important and time-consuming blessing of a new baby. Nalin Ranasinghe's conversation and encouragement were both lively and valuable. Provost Francis Lazarus of Assumption College provided support that enabled me to complete the manuscript in a timely fashion. Several Assumption colleagues offered incisive suggestions at a faculty symposium.

R. Shep Melnick provided extensive and immensely helpful comments on the manuscript. James Patterson, whose published Moynihan scholarship was of itself a sufficient influence, was also kind enough to offer detailed remarks on sections of the project. Judge Robert Katzmann of the Second Circuit Court of Appeals, a longtime Moynihan associate and his former teaching assistant at Harvard, was generous with counsel amid what I can only assume was an overwhelming schedule. Moynihan's close friend George F. Will shared his insights and in particular accentuated the distinction between New Deal and Great Society liberalism. Richard Reinsch of the indispensable Liberty Fund's indispensable Online Library of Law and Liberty published pieces on Moynihan that allowed me to road test some of the ideas that appear here. Peter Skerry's memories and insights were of great assistance. Sandor Karz was an invaluable research assistant at several stages of the project. Jessica Heywood and Nicholas Feld faithfully and rapidly transcribed an ungodly amount of notes. Carey introduced me to Burke and served as a sounding board in the initial research phases before his death, which so many of us still grieve, in the summer of 2013. His wife, Claire, has continued to be a source of professional encouragement and personal friendship. Martin and Phyllis Weiner yet again offered up their home and their parental pampering as I wrote. My brother Zach Weinersmith, as skilled a writer as I know, edited the manuscript as well.

For my wife, Rebecca, and my children, Hannah, Jacob, and Theodore—whose attempted interactions with me were for many months foiled by the attention I fixed on a computer screen in the predawn and postdinner hours—there is, as with the last book, neither adequate gratitude nor adequate love. But in limitless quantities, they have both.

American Burke

Introduction:
"And You Still Break Stone"

Jimmy Carter may have had the nation right, but if he meant to include Senator Daniel Patrick Moynihan in his diagnosis of malaise in the much-derided "Crisis of Confidence" address he delivered on July 15, 1979, he got the gentleman from New York dead wrong. Touched by experience with a sense of the tragic in politics, Moynihan nonetheless clung to a stubborn optimism about its possibilities. But those possibilities were bounded by a defining feature of his politics: limitation. There were limits to what government could do and, more important, limits to how it should attempt to do it. Government, he said more than once, was good at redistributing wealth and power—a worthy goal to which Moynihan, a New Deal liberal, adhered—but incompetent at carrying out a range of activities it had undertaken, providing services at ever more microscopic levels foremost among them. A cleavage had opened inside liberal thought between those who saw the state as the sole engine of progress and those who believed politics could help nourish "an essential diversity in American life" through which the goals of liberal politics were attained not merely by the state but also by the vast, voluntary sector of what Alexis de Tocqueville identified as civic associations. When Moynihan ascended a podium to give a little-noticed but insightful speech to the United Way of America in New York City eight days after Carter's address, he meant to explain the distinction.

"The President is right to speak to us of a crisis of morale in our society, and we owe him our gratitude for putting this subject at the center of public discourse," Moynihan said. "But we also owe him our help in understanding its causes," one of which was the conquest of the private sector by the public sector—something that Joseph A. Schumpeter had predicted and that Moynihan was fond of citing.[1] This was a proper topic not merely of right-left debate but also of discussion within the parameters of liberal thought, for there are indeed two traditions and outlooks which intermingle under the broad canopy of what we frequently characterize as "liberalism."

One of these I [have] called the pluralist position. It is a view held by those who, with Edmund Burke, believe that . . . the nature of man is intricate; the objects of society are of the greatest possible complexity; and therefore no simple disposition or direction of power can be suitable either to man's nature or to the quality of his affairs. . . . These liberals hold that between the individual and the state is to be found a great and beneficent array of social and economic entities. They believe that in the strength of these voluntary, private associations—church, family, club, trade union, commercial association—lies much of the strength of democratic society.[2]

Here was Moynihan acknowledging a central feature of his politics: the inherent complexity of human society and, therefore, the danger of being seduced by what he called "simplism."[3] He often quoted scientist and systems analyst Jay W. Forrester's maxim that "with a high degree of confidence we can say that the intuitive solution to the problems of complex social systems will be wrong most of the time." Yet crucially, Moynihan would add, this "need not be a traumatizing truth"; it might instead be an enlightening, even empowering, one.[4] Similarly, Peter H. Rossi's "Iron Law of Evaluation"—"that," in Moynihan's words, "the expected value for any measured effect of a social program is zero"—"is not a counsel of despair. It is useful knowledge."[5] When his lifelong collaborator Nathan Glazer, the sociologist, wrote what seemed to be a grim book about the possibilities of social policy, Moynihan accepted the limits his friend identified, but his jacket blurb viewed them capaciously nonetheless: "Yes, there are limits, but they are well beyond our present horizons. Glazer summons us to try once more, and to do better this time."[6]

Perhaps because he appreciated such limits, Moynihan—the author of dozens of articles and author, coauthor, or editor of nineteen books (more, his friend George F. Will once remarked, than most senators had read)—possessed an uncanny ability to conceptualize problems in transformative ways. In his imagination, traffic safety became a matter of epidemiology, secrecy a form of regulation. Guns didn't kill people, bullets did. The problem of welfare was not poverty but dependency. Society was "defining deviancy down"—reclassifying formerly deviant behavior as normal so as not to exceed its quota of abhorrence. A Socratic gadfly who saw his role as challenging orthodoxy wherever it reigned—Moynihan would elucidate government's limits during periods of Democratic rule and defend its possibilities under Republicans—he now applied that skill at defining problems to the crisis that was cleaving liberalism. He continued in the 1979 United Way remarks:

> This pluralistic strain of liberalism may be contrasted to another which I [have] described as "statist." The term sounds rather more invidious than I intend it—for I well recall the time when it seemed that industrial democracies could endure and progress only through a massive expansion of government involvement in their institutional arrangements. . . . But today we are also beginning to see evidence of overreliance upon the state as an instrument for improving the commonweal. We see it in the unsteady condition of the family, we see it in the erosion of private education, we see it in the bureaucratic chill that pervades so many of our government agencies, we see it in the faltering sense of neighborhood in our urban centers, we see it even, one might argue, in the awesome decline of citizen participation in our elections. For, again in Edmund Burke's much-quoted words, "to be attached to the subdivisions, to love the little platoon we belong to in society, is the first principle (germ as it were) of public affections."

Moynihan's complaint lay with Carter's implicit claim that objecting to lodging further power with the state constituted selfishness and risked, in the president's term, "fragmentation." Yet Moynihan rejected with equal force the idea that politics had no role to play in social progress. The risk of state conquest of intermediary institutions was that "the web of family, church, civic and ethnic association, neighborhood and school, through which the individual is linked to the larger institutions of government and the economy" would be strained to the point that there would be "no buffer between the individual and the state." Crucially, however, "these institutions can be strengthened only when government and the 'third sector' cooperate to nurture them." Hence, Moynihan proposed, along with his longtime friend Senator Bob Packwood, an Oregon Republican, to allow individuals who did not itemize deductions to deduct charitable contributions on their tax returns. The expansion of the standard deduction had diminished the incentive for contributions from the average family, he elsewhere explained, transforming the character of intermediary institutions by compelling them to rely increasingly on the privileged.[7] He continued: "The way to the unity we now seek and need does not lie in railing against pluralism, a note that can be heard in castigations of 'fragmentation' or 'narrow interests.' The way to unity lies in an acknowledgment of the legitimacy of differences, and an understanding that the art of politics consists of drawing them into a harmony that, if not always magnificent, at least is widely acceptable."

The remarks are worth extended reflection, but not because they constitute a Rosetta stone for Moynihan's thinking, which was too nuanced, complex, and vast for a single key to unlock. His experience itself was too diverse to be simply deciphered: aide to Governor Averell Harriman of New York; assistant secretary of labor to Presidents John F. Kennedy (JFK) and Lyndon B. Johnson (LBJ); White House counselor to President Richard Nixon; US ambassador to India and the United Nations; US senator; and, between it all, a sometime professor and frequent scholar whose published works would have marked him as a first-rate political thinker had he never taken an oath to preserve, protect, and defend the Constitution.

Rather, the United Way remarks warrant analysis because they illustrate the unique character of Moynihan's political thought, which is properly located on the liberal stratum—but a strain of liberalism largely lost since his death in 2003. Moynihan's liberalism, which I shall argue bears striking affinities to the political thought of Edmund Burke (though I do not mean to trace a genealogy to him), is a politics of both possibility and limitation, one constrained by a respect for social complexity, empirical circumstance, and private association. But it is also a politics of mutual endeavor, one that sees elected government as "the instrument of the common purpose of a free people; [one that] can embrace great causes; and do great things."[8]

These positions have broken largely along left-right dichotomies in contemporary politics. We are accustomed to the assumption that liberals defend the public sector, conservatives the private; that liberals pursue bold solutions while conservatives warn of complex systems and unanticipated consequences. That one person might hew to both sides and do so consistently seems alien to our discourse. But there is no contradiction here. On the contrary, there is deep complementarity between the ideas of possibility, on the one hand, and limitation, on the other, between private pluralism and common purpose. Burke, a conserving reformer, embodied both. So did Moynihan, an unrelenting devotee of the New Deal yet an occasional critic of the Great Society, a Cold Warrior eloquent in his denunciations of totalitarianism yet equally stirring as a champion of international law, a fierce defender of welfare yet an innovative leader in its reform. The claim here is not that Moynihan found a balance between the values of possibility and limitation—a sort of centrism of accommodation—but rather that he maintained, and that it is both possible and admirable to maintain, a deep and simultaneous commitment to both. Limitation grounds possibility in the concrete and the real. Pluralism, on Moynihan's account, magnifies and multiplies what politics alone can achieve. This conviction was reflected in his deep and oft-stated commitment to the Catholic principle of subsidiarity, the belief that a social problem should be addressed by the closest competent institution to it.

This commitment to both vibrant public authority and the preservation of the private sphere is equally evident in his beliefs in constitutionalism and the dispersal and separation of powers, shown in his fierce commitment as a senator to the prerogatives of the institution in which he served for four terms. He was a defender of a strong presidency but also of a robust Congress that maintained a proper constitutional balance. He crusaded against government secrecy that, among other ails, inflated executive power. One of the benefits of international law, he argued, was that it would ground foreign policy in something other than free-ranging executive will.

That contemporary politics leaves little room for so broad and imaginative an account of politics as Moynihan's is evidence of what he, following his friend the sociologist Daniel Bell, called the "exhaustion of political ideas."[9] It also explains why he defies labels or, put otherwise, why our contemporary labels—as narrow as our imagination—defy him. But there was one label he welcomed consistently: liberal. By this, he referred to the conviction that government had the responsibility to ameliorate economic distress and the capacity to enhance civic life. Moynihan once said of Michael Oakeshott—whose lectures he attended as a student at the London School of Economics and whom he admired—that he "was not so much a conservative in his desires for society as in his expectations of it."[10] One may say of Moynihan that he was a liberal not so much in his expectations for government as in his hopes for it. But limits inherently circumscribed politics. Thus, Moynihan observed,

> the matter comes to this. The stability of a democracy depends very much on the people making a careful distinction between what government can do and what it cannot do. To demand what can be done is altogether in order: some may wish such things accomplished, some may not, and the majority may decide. But to seek that which cannot be provided, especially to do so with the passionate but misinformed conviction that it can be, is to create the conditions of frustration and ruin.[11]

Still, limitation was no excuse for stasis. He could reflect (and not approvingly) that Oakeshott "was conservative almost to the point of passivity."[12] Knowledge of one's limits was useful as a principle of action, not indifference. Knowing what one could not do illuminated what one could, and politics could accomplish plenty. The New Deal had. Moynihan's objection lay with the shift that occurred in liberal thinking somewhere between the New Deal and the Great Society.[13] The New Deal offered amelioration, at which government was good because government was good at raising revenue and cutting checks. The Great Society offered programs around which constituencies—often professional, middle-class groups with interests distinct from those of the people the programs were intended to help—accreted. They micromanaged; they agitated; they were envious of nonstate actors.

Moynihan flatly rejected what he regarded as the demonstrably false thesis that the Great Society in any sense "caused" the social dysfunction in poor communities, pathologies he had diagnosed before the Great Society was ever conceived. But he nonetheless came to see its piecemeal, programmatic approach as fatally flawed. Among those flaws was the Great Society's rejection of the politics of limitation. Moynihan himself emerged chastened from the experience of Johnson's War on Poverty and even, to some extent, from the boundless hopefulness of Kennedy's New Frontier. This sense of limitation was nowhere more evident than in his appreciation for the boundaries of empirical circumstance. "Everyone is entitled to his own opinion," he famously and frequently said, "but not his own facts." Echoing Burke's skepticism of abstraction, he once complained that the testimony of a witness before a Senate committee had "all the clarity of logic but none of the fuzziness and grit and dirt and detail of reality."[14] An accomplished social scientist, Moynihan bore high hopes for the capacity of social science to inform social policy. But pivotally for understanding his appreciation of the limitations of circumstance, this role was to be *retrospective* and evaluative—that is, grounded in specific circumstance—not prospective and abstract. Grandiose vision was less important in governing than a little bit of foresight; the art of politics "is not that of prophesying, but of coping." But again, he added the crucial caveat: "This is no timorous exercise, much less a surrender to expediency," a reminder that recalls Burke's dictum that prudence requires its own courage.[15] For Moynihan, this knowledge of limits was, or ought to have been, the basis of constructive activity grounded in the knowledge that "social change, as seen from the perspective of history, comes slowly, one step at a time, from the point of view of the individual demanding it."[16]

Understanding limitation, he rejected radical moralization and total politicization, especially the variant that infected left-wing politics in the 1960s. This sanctimonious politics "rewarded the articulation of moral purpose more than the achievement of practical good."[17] In speaking of this strain of the American Left and its intolerance of dissent, he referred often to Hannah Arendt's insight that totalitarian propagandists succeeded in turning every question of fact into one of motive. The author of the much and often unfairly maligned Moynihan Report on the plight of the African American family knew of what he spoke.

But his disgust with the radicals of the 1960s has been misconstrued as alienation from the New Deal liberalism from which they, in fact, were alienated and from which he himself never varied. Moynihan's thought, to be sure, is tinged throughout with references to conservative thinkers—more often, perhaps, than liberal ones. Oakeshott's appearances are frequent. Robert A. Nisbet, too, comes on stage, and Burke is an occasional character as well. John Rawls, to my knowledge, is not to be found. The temptation is to assume a strain of conservatism in Moynihan's thinking, but this can be misleading for several reasons. One is that Moynihan's intellectual curiosity was such that he gravitated toward thinkers with whom he disagreed precisely because he disagreed with them and could consequently learn from them.

The second is that Moynihan identified many of the relevant ideas as liberal, not conservative, as in "the liberal tradition of respect for facts," the liberal belief in "restraint" and the "persistence of sin," or the claim that "the doctrines of liberalism are derived from experience, rather than right reason."[18] Third, he explicitly rejected the conservative label most often applied to him—neoconservative—as having been "coined in epithet." It applies defensibly to thinkers such as Irving Kristol who turned from their liberal commitments. Moynihan never did. He joined the Nixon White House not out of frustration with liberals but rather out of an intuition—correct, as it turned out—that the Republican administration would provide a forward-moving vehicle for his liberal ambitions.[19] Finally, a thinker of Moynihan's self-awareness is entitled to self-description, and his was, repeatedly and without any exception of which I am aware, liberal.[20]

Still, he has had his critics, especially from the left—in 1979, an entire issue of the *Nation,* intended to scuttle a falsely rumored Moynihan presidential bid, called him everything from a conservative to a "clown"—but also from the right. They have called him a chameleon whose political ideals morphed in appearance to suit either side. Neoconservatives from Norman Podhoretz to Elliot Abrams have said his liberal rhetoric was borne of political expediency.[21]

There are limits to the extent to which these tensions can be resolved—and, for that matter, limits to which they should even be understood as critiques. Moynihan was less a chameleon than a man who occupied different roles at different times. The natural caution of a scholar can be lethal to the policy ambitions of a statesman. Political actors pushing policy programs must back them boldly; scholars evaluating policy programs must trim to the constant awareness of alternative explanations. As a senator, Moynihan once wrote that he was, on a given topic, "enter[ing] the realm of speculation, from which, perhaps, no scholarly reputation ever returns. But that is not a choice available in politics. Speculate or perish."[22] Statesmen who seek to act must experiment. For a scholar, "Rossi's law" is a penetrating insight; for a politician, it can be, as Moynihan said, "useful knowledge"; but rigidly followed, it would also be a formula for quietism.

Senator Moynihan was given to generalizations to which Professor Moynihan, especially were he seeking tenure in a modern department of political science, might have been averse. Some of Moynihan's most interesting insights arose from his years out of government and in the academy—the time of his book *Coping: On the Practice of Government.* This was a period of skepticism and probing, qualities less available (though hardly inaccessible) to the politician undertaking forward-leaning action. Moynihan's shifting roles even within his space as a statesman must also be understood. He was a frequent policy maker but a sometime gadfly; in the latter role, he likely often stated his criticisms provocatively precisely in order to provoke. In no case do I suggest that Moynihan did not mean what he said, only that the context of what he said matters.

Still, this study will suggest that these left-right critiques of Moynihan—liberals who thought he was a conservative and conservatives who saw matters the other way around—might be more deeply resolved by understanding him on his own terms. I will also assert that there is a lens through which his particular strain of liberalism can be consistently understood. I shall call it "Burkean liberalism"—not, again, to claim any particular influence of Burke on Moynihan but rather to accentuate both its uniqueness and, since Moynihan's death, its absence. The idea of Burkean liberalism as Moynihan embodied it is this: government should do forthrightly that which government is capable of doing. He construed this expansively, and this is what made him a liberal. Government was capable of redistributing wealth, of shaping conditions that would encourage family cohesion, of conquering poverty understood as material privation, of waging ideological battle against totalitarianism, and more. Similarly, government should do thoughtfully what it could not avoid doing, which included erecting public architecture, enacting policies that affected families, and interacting with other world powers in ideological forums.

But politics ought to be aware of its own limitations. Moynihan was, and this is what marks his affinity with Burke. He believed that politics should be grounded in the concrete, not the abstract, and that it should not promise what it could not deliver. It ought to hold sacrosanct the meaning of words, the currency of political exchange. And it should be grounded in the traditional structures of society—Burke's "little platoons," a phrase that Moynihan particularly favored—that serve as the foundation of political society. Politics ought to respect social complexity.

This appreciation of complexity led Moynihan, like Burke, to reject ideology. In 1994, a *New York Times* reporter asked him to describe his "credo." He replied: "Nothing I want to give a name to. I'm not a Socialist and I'm not a Libertarian. I was never a Stalinist and I was never a Trotskyite. I guess if I had to say—and I don't have to say, but you asked—it's an avoidance of ideology."[23] For him, ideology was a corrupting force, one that excessively simplified complex situations and subjugated the constraints of circumstance to sweeping political goals. "Ideological certainty," he once wrote in scolding the Clinton administration, "easily degenerates into an insistence upon ignorance."[24] Virtue—a device on which he recognized the American constitutional regime did not readily rely—could be necessary to restrain it.[25]

Ideology led, moreover, to the false seduction of grandiose promises, such as the Reagan administration's belief that lower taxes would lead to higher revenues or the Gingrich Republicans' view that the experience of poverty could be transformed through severe treatment of welfare recipients. Moynihan had seen such promises made and go unmet in the 1960s: the result was not merely disillusionment but charges of ill intent, the disease of distrust thereby infecting the body politic. He observed, "The polity must take care what it undertakes to provide, for failure to do so is likely to be attributed to malevolent purpose. This is not to say expectations should not be raised, but only that they should not be raised indiscriminately."[26]

Thus his fondness for William Butler Yeats's "Parnell," the poetic plea for limits that Moynihan described as the only twentieth-century political verse worth remembering: "Parnell came down the road, he said to a cheering man: / 'Ireland shall get her freedom and you still break stone.'"[27] There were no utopian solutions in politics; there was no single stroke of state that would transform every life. Such is the essence of the politics of limits, the basis of a Burkean liberalism. But there is one more thing to say about breaking stone: it is not a futile endeavor. Neither, for Moynihan, was politics. Undertaken over a lifetime, with a steadiness and relentlessness of purpose appropriate to a thinker whose adventures ranged from the Kennedy administration to the United Nations to the US Senate—on topics as various as poverty, nuclear arms control, the law of nations, ethnicity, governmental secrecy, and beyond—its achievement can be immense. Moynihan's was.

1. The Central Truths

The central conservative truth is that it is culture, not politics, that determines the success of a society. The central liberal truth is that politics can change a culture and save it from itself. Witness the civil rights legislation of the 1960s that conservatives so opposed.

—Moynihan, *Family and Nation*, 1986

THE POLITICS OF LIMITATION

Daniel Patrick Moynihan arrived in John F. Kennedy's Washington a political idealist and left Lyndon B. Johnson's administration a chastened man. Remarkably few fundamental shifts are detectable in Moynihan's thought over the course of his career—not that these would be troubling in the thinking of someone constrained by empirical circumstance, which necessarily evolves—but this was one. Something happened; as his friend the chemist and philosopher Michael Polanyi said in one of Moynihan's favorite aphorisms, "People change their minds."

Just after he left the Johnson administration and before he began publicly to criticize the War on Poverty's approach, Moynihan had penned the lead article for the inaugural edition of *Public Interest*, entitled "The Professionalization of Reform." He wrote with a breezy confidence befitting the New Frontier. Between John Maynard Keynes and econometrics, the business cycle had been conquered. Social reform was now the province of professional experts, and the War on Poverty was its latest iteration. This professionalization was, he observed, "a technique that will not appeal to everyone, and in which many will perceive the not altogether imaginary danger of a too powerful government. But it is also a technique that offers a profound promise of social sanity and stability in time to come." The cost would be "a decline in the moral exhilaration of public affairs at the domestic level," yet the professionalization of reform also held out the possibility of "the creation of a society that can put an end to the 'animal miseries' and stupid controversies that afflict most peoples."[1]

By the late 1960s, however, violence was erupting in the nation's cities, and the Great Society was foundering on the shoals of interest group liberalism and inadequate resources. Moynihan—now out of government and in the academy, which gave him a perspective that naturally evoked a greater emphasis on limitation—had acquired (or at least was newly emphasizing) a sense of the complexity of political endeavor.[2] He reflected later: "In the mid-1960s, when I began writing again, I had considerably scaled down my expectations of what government could do about most things—in the early 1960s in Washington we thought we could do anything, and we found out different—and had acquired the discipline of not being too much impressed by clever-seeming people."[3]

He would write of this period: "American liberalism had, in those years, lost a sense of limits. We would transform the Mekong Delta, resurrect Detroit, enlighten South Asia and defend it too, for that matter."[4] He would recall that "the presidential advisers of the Kennedy and Johnson era had underestimated the difficulties of social change . . . a naiveté born of noble purpose. The limits of policy were less and less emphasized while the potential for matters to get worse rather than better was increasingly ignored."[5]

This chapter proposes a framework for how Moynihan's political thought can be understood—as a blend of hues associated with both liberalism (possibilities linked with governmental action) and conservatism (limitations born of respect for social complexity) to form a unique shade of political thought. Viewing Moynihan through this prism enables us to appreciate both the originality of his ideas and, importantly, their mutual appeal to liberals and conservatives, an appeal that has led both sides to lay dueling claims to his legacy. Liberals and conservatives certainly have much about which to disagree, but Moynihan's thought shows their mistake in assuming that these beliefs—aspiration and limitation, respectively—cannot be simultaneously held.

Moynihan the liberal believed in shared endeavor pursued through the mechanism of government; at the same time, he appreciated the limits that social complexity imposed.

It is essential to emphasize at the outset that the labels "liberal" and "conservative" were less important to Moynihan and are less important to this study than the ideas themselves. As we shall see, Moynihan associated both possibility and limitation in key respects with liberalism. Our concern lies more with the unique brew that arose from this blend rather than with the names applied to the ingredients. We begin with the decisive significance, evident in multiple contexts throughout Moynihan's thought, of limitation.

Limitation

For Moynihan, all human endeavor, especially that undertaken politically, was subject to limitation. We might trace this commitment to any number of sources—the Catholic doctrine of fallen man, Burke's warnings of the limits of reason, or simple commonsense observation—but it was there. There were limits to the capacity of human beings to manipulate infinitely intricate social systems and limits to the ability of reason fully to comprehend them. For Moynihan, this theme found its most deeply reflective expression in the long introduction to his 1973 book *Coping: On the Practice of Government*, a collection of writings reflecting perhaps his most theoretically fruitful period, that arising from his contemplation of the promise and shortfalls of the 1960s.

> Increasingly it is what is known about life that makes it problematical. The dictum of Ecclesiastes 1:18, "For in much wisdom is much grief and he that increaseth knowledge increaseth sorrow," seems more fitted to our time; and education is more and more a matter of coming to terms with this less optimistic vision. . . . The unexpected, the unforeseen: the public life of our age seems dominated by events of this cast, while the task of intellect seems increasingly that of imposing some measure of order on this less than cosmic chaos. After a period of chiliastic vision we have

entered a time that requires a more sober assessment of our chances, and a more modest approach to events.[6]

The problem, he reflected, was that the brand of radical politics that came to characterize the expectations of the 1960s not only mistrusted but also actively resisted gradual reform: "It is the seeming nature of the chiliast to resist social changes which, however profound, are not perceived as somehow ultimate."[7] Moynihan, by contrast, imposed the constraints of limitation on the idealist impulses of liberalism. Politicians could not be subject to a religious requirement of purity. "Their achievements can never be more than relatively good," he said, expressing an idea with echoes of both Burke, for whom politics was always a choice between lesser goods, and Oakeshott, for whom it was tinged with a permanently tragic dimension.[8] Politics in a democracy seemed to require heart-quickening causes for sustenance. Prudence, however, was difficult to communicate. "It was easy to be captain of the *Indomitable*, was it not? But what commands," he asked, "shall issue forth from the quarterdeck of the *Worried*, the *Uncertain*, the *Not Sure.*"[9] Moynihan imagined a newly inaugurated President Kennedy standing on the windswept front of the US Capitol and stirring a nation with words of prudent perspective: "'So let every nation know that we would be crazy to undertake to pay any price, bear any burden, meet any hardship, support any friend, oppose any foe to assure the survival and success of liberty.' . . . No, there would have been nothing inspiring in this. There might also have been no Vietnam."[10]

This appreciation for limits must not be mistaken for quietism. Moynihan remained an advocate of muscular government, but he also noted that "having through all my adult life worked to make the American national government larger, stronger, more active, I nonetheless plead that there are limits to what it may be asked to do."[11] It was, to repeat, imperative to separate what government could competently do from what it could not—as much to ensure government *did* competently what it could do as to prevent it from undertaking the impossible.

In the 1960s, the sociologist James Coleman led what was then and still may be the largest social science experiment ever undertaken—a study of the effect of various inputs on educational outcomes. Its results showed the primacy of family structure, nearly to the exclusion of other variables such as per pupil expenditure.[12] Moynihan recalled the political scientist Seymour Martin Lipset approaching him at the Harvard Faculty Club and asking if he had heard about Coleman's findings: "And I said, 'What?' And he said, 'All family.' And I said, 'Oh God.' We both looked at Coleman's influential study with consternation about the relative incapacity it revealed of public institutions to shape individuals."[13] His disquietude, which Coleman shared, pertained to a realization of the expanding scope of limitation,[14] but note his use of the word *relative*. Moynihan was not denying government's ability to shape individual behavior. The point was that government could not simply do what it did best—spend money—and expect educational outcomes to follow. This was different, it is crucial to observe, from saying government could not do anything.

But government had to appreciate what it could not do in order to undertake successfully what it could. Moynihan attended Oakeshott's inaugural lecture when the British philosopher succeeded Harold Laski in a professorial chair at the London School of Economics, and he would recur to it often. "Oakeshott preached the art of the possible, and bespoke the fate of those who reject those limitations: 'To try to do something which is inherently impossible is always a corrupting enterprise.'"[15] In a 1969 commencement address at the University of Notre Dame, Moynihan reflected:

> What is it that government cannot provide? It cannot provide values to persons who have none, or who have lost those they had. It cannot provide a meaning to life. It cannot provide inner peace. It can provide outlets for moral energies, but it cannot create those energies. In particular, government cannot cope with the crisis in values that is sweeping the Western world. It cannot respond to the fact that so many of our young people do not believe what those before them have believed, do not accept the authority of

institutions and customs whose authority has heretofore been accepted, do not embrace or even very much like the culture that they inherit.[16]

Notice Moynihan's concern here with the collapse of social authority—an appreciation for the necessity of society's intermediate institutions. He would allude more than once to Nisbet's observation that a vacuum of authority cleared the path for raw power. We also see in the passage that the politics of limitation must recognize space for morality.[17] This was, crucially, *private* space: space in the social sphere. Its misdirection into the realm of politics was one of the pathologies of the 1960s, whose overly moralized politics descended into an all-consuming Manichaeism. Late in that decade, Moynihan wrote of a religious crisis in which the essentially spiritual cravings of the time were channeled instead into politics. The "principal issues of the moment" were only "*seen*" as political; that they were was "the essential clue as to their nature. But the crisis of the time is not political, it is in essence religious. It is a religious crisis of large numbers of intensely moral, even godly, people who no longer hope for God."[18] The absence of spirituality was akin to the absence of authority, for it left a gap in private space that, when not nourished by intermediate institutions, was filled, unhealthily, by politics. The resulting "fervor becomes pathological" and leads to "the total state; the politicization of all things."[19] This was evident in the tendency of 1960s radicals to regard all disputes as political disputes and thus see anyone with whom they disagreed about anything as a political enemy.

Still, even while resisting politicization, Moynihan defended government. When, paraphrasing Reinhold Niebuhr, he said that failing to "accept that there are some things that can't be changed, and learning to recognize which they are" was "to be false to a large vocation,"[20] he meant to identify some limits as permanent and grounded in the nature of things, not merely in circumstance, but he also meant to defend the vocation. When Carter argued that government could not "eliminate poverty, provide a bountiful economy, reduce inflation, save our cities, cure illiteracy, provide energy, or mandate goodness," Moynihan responded that the president had gone "farther than I would": "For the government can eliminate poverty—that is, poverty defined as income below a certain level. A good welfare reform bill would do that. This is precisely the kind of thing government can succeed in doing. It cannot 'mandate goodness.' But it can 'save our cities'—if not from sin, then surely from bankruptcy."[21] By the early 1980s, he was worried about an overcorrection in the Reagan era. "We have moved far too precipitously and blindly," he said, "from sublime confidence in government to solve all our problems and meet all our needs to what can only be termed a profound mistrust of government's ability to do anything at all."[22]

Moynihan's appreciation for limits was inextricably linked to his recognition of the complexity of the social organism and the inherent difficulty of manipulating it politically. Here, we arrive at a decisive supposition for Moynihan's thought and, especially, the character of it that blends a Burkean perspective into his liberal one. Like Burke—again, the claim is compatibility, not influence—Moynihan accepted the limitations that complexity imposed on human understanding and the human capacity to manipulate social mechanisms. Social problems tended to be "counter-intuitive," resistant to simple solutions, precisely because "they arise out of complex systems" rather than "simple loop systems."

> A while back, one of Harvard's great chemists was discoursing on what he called the "many-body problem," a condition in which the number of variables interacting with one another in any given situation makes that situation extraordinarily complicated and difficult to fathom. I asked in what range of numbers this "many-body problem" begins. A somehow suspicious glance was returned. Did I really not know? Apparently not. "Three," he replied.
>
> This is an aspect of our reality.[23]

The problem was the tendency of democratic peoples to insist on simplicity and to be willing to pay a high price to retain the illusion of it. But matters for Moynihan were rarely simple, least of all in social policy, and he believed liberals in particular bore a responsibility for recognizing that complexity and the limitations it imposed. As such, it was a particular source of consternation for him when conservatives, rather than liberals, showed appreciation for it. In July 1993, frustrated with the moralism of the newly installed Clinton administration, he exchanged letters with the president's economic adviser, Laura D'Andrea Tyson. Tyson had just attended a Senate Democratic caucus meeting and claimed that studies supported the administration's request for millions of dollars for a favored program. "Just for fun," in Moynihan's words, he requested two citations to back up her claim. In his letter to Tyson, he noted the administration's propensity to claim "with great vigor that something or other is known in an area of social policy which, to the best of my understanding, is not known at all." Then came the warning: "The great strength of political conservatives at this time (and for a generation) is that they are open to the thought that matters are complex. Liberals have got into a reflexive pattern of denying this. I had hoped twelve years in the wilderness might have changed this; it may be it has only reinforced it. If this is so, the current revival of liberalism will be brief and inconsequential."[24] Precisely because the complexity of society imposed limits on the aspirations of politics, government had to take care not to promise more than it could deliver. As he put it, "Wisdom surely bespeaks moderation in promises of the future, and restraint in its promises for it."[25]

Complexity, like limitation, did not necessarily counsel inaction; it might actually permit boldness. Indeed, Moynihan's respect for limitation was bounded by the fact that he could be a proponent of bold strokes. The guaranteed income was certainly one such stroke, and his support for it challenges the image of him as rejecting single-shot solutions to complex problems. Still, even as the requirements of political life forced him to a boldness that Moynihan the scholar might have questioned, he worked to keep expectations for government within reasonable bounds. At a Senate hearing on welfare in 1977, for example, he reviewed a series of reform proposals undertaken over the previous decade. "I do not contend that all of these proposals were good," he said.

"But I must paraphrase Michael Oakeshott and say, 'Politics is not the art of building a perfect society; it is the art of making improvements.'"[26]

This respect for social complexity is among the reasons Moynihan preferred what he called "policy liberalism" to "program liberalism." Policy liberalism, by which government would define a goal and pursue it across an integrated range of programmatic and policy vehicles, recognized the complexity and interrelatedness of social systems. Program liberalism, by contrast, erected narrow programs and proceeded, interest groups and all, to defend them. Aid to Families with Dependent Children (AFDC) was a program. By contrast, a family *policy* would establish family stability as an overriding national goal and seek to coordinate the vast array of federal programs and policies affecting families, from taxes to welfare, and direct them toward that objective.

The defining feature of the policy approach was its appreciation for the complexity of things. But observe that it is precisely that awareness of complexity that, in this case, counsels comprehensive rather than gradual solutions. "Knowing what we do about the nature of society and of social interventions, we have no option but to seek to deal in terms of the entire society, and all the consequences of intervention," Moynihan wrote, expressing in a single sentence both an awareness of complexity and a willingness to proceed boldly.[27] Discrete programs, however, accrued interests of their own—entities and individuals, often quite distinct from the actual constituencies of the programs themselves, that benefited from the programs and proceeded to resist any change; sometimes, they even insisted their own efforts had failed in order to maintain their funding. Moynihan observed, "For some, social legislation can have the effect of narcotic drugs on the addict: Ever-stronger doses are required."[28]

Given the fact of complexity, politics had to be tethered to empirical circumstance. Circumstances bounded political experience and imposed the limitation Moynihan felt was necessary to the success of political endeavor. Consequently, just as Burke had refused to consider anything in the "nakedness of metaphysical abstraction," Moynihan believed in a politics rooted in experience.[29] From Edward Gibbon's *Decline and Fall of the Roman Empire*, he borrowed the notion of a "leakage of reality" and applied it in several contexts.[30] He admired the Founders' "new science of politics" for its retrospective rather than prospective basis: "Read *The Federalist Papers*, the work of Madison, Hamilton, and Jay, and you will know a lot about America. Read Lenin and you will know a lot about Russia. If you do both, you will note how very much more the Soviet system is based on prophecies about future events in this world."[31] The Founders, facing a crisis of the old European order, adapted to it. By contrast, their French revolutionary counterparts attempted root and branch to undo it, Moynihan wrote in a passage that might easily be mistaken for Burke's *Reflections*, "as, for example, when they changed the names of the days of the week and declared 1792 to be *L'année Une*. Year One."[32] The emphasis on empirical evidence was not a dictum to which the constraints of politics always permitted Moynihan to adhere—the guaranteed income, again, though rooted in social scientific thinking, can nonetheless be seen as a large-scale experiment—but it was generally present in his thought.

This appreciation of limitation in politics contextualizes Moynihan's views on the appropriate role for social science in informing public policy, demonstrating, as well, the unique blend of aspiration and limitation in his politics. On the one hand, Moynihan, an accomplished social scientist, held considerable hopes for his chosen field's practical applications. On the other hand, one of the faults of the early 1960s was an excessive faith in expertise, including on Moynihan's part. "I have been guilty," he admitted, "of optimism about the use of social-science knowledge in the management of public affairs."[33] The solution was to turn social science backward, toward experience, rather than forward, toward abstract prophecy: "Social science is at its weakest, at its worst, when it offers theories of individual or collective behavior which raise the possibility, by controlling certain inputs, of bringing about mass behavioral change. No such knowledge now exists."[34] Instead, "*the role of social science lies not in the formulation of social policy, but in the measurement of its results.* The great questions of government have to do not with what *will* work, but with what *does* work."³⁵ Moynihan sounded clearly Burkean in warning against "the increasing introduction into politics and government of ideas originating in the social sciences which promise to bring about social change through the manipulation of what might be termed the hidden processes of society."³⁶

Social scientists, who tended to be politically liberal, ran aground when they pursued public policies out of personal proclivities. Yet woe betide the social scientist who dared to present evidence at odds with prevailing political preferences. Moynihan went so far as to suggest— "seriously," he claimed—that "the training of social scientists in years to come should include something equivalent to the processes by which psychiatrists are taught to anticipate and accept hostility."³⁷ In any event, "social scientists worthy of the name will call 'em as they see 'em, and this can produce no end of outrage at the plate, or in the stands."³⁸

This respect for empirical circumstance was, for Moynihan, a *liberal* value, one uniquely required to ground liberal goals. Liberals in particular, precisely because they wanted government to work well, would respect empirical circumstance as a limiting condition on their aspirations. "Government, especially liberal government, that would attempt many things very much needs the discipline of skeptical and complex intelligence repeatedly inquiring 'What do you mean?' and 'How do you know?' The expectations of such government need to be controlled by insights such as Nisbet's on the unlikelihood of final social peace."³⁹ Respecting the complexity of society would often mean acknowledging ignorance. Consequently, social scientists would increasingly be called upon to "assert the absence of knowledge" on urgent issues.⁴⁰

However, this reliance on empirical fact and the acceptance of ignorance did not comprise a "formula for immobilism." John F. Kennedy and Eugene McCarthy had shared a belief in relying on social science, and they could hardly be so accused. "But both [were] men whose minds were touched by a certain sadness at having perceived the complexity and difficulty of it all: both men for whom the achievement of limited goals lacked nothing in glory."⁴¹ For a political actor, as opposed to a scholar, immobilism was no option. Indeed, knowing what one did not know could help to isolate and identify what one did, and in the process, it could inform constructive action. The following passage thus discusses ignorance in terms of constructive *uses* directed toward initiative: "The uses of ignorance—acknowledged, understood ignorance—are many, and one can imagine in the decade ahead that social science proceeding from these premises can help to impose a desperately needed discipline on the way we discuss social issues, and the programs we devise to deal with them."[42] Precisely because Moynihan supported the broad range of liberal goals that society had set, he asserted that "an unflinching insistence on fact [would] be a major asset."[43]

The Politics of Pluralism

The complexity of society counseled against centralization because the premise of the latter was based on the capacity of planners and policy makers at the center to impose solutions that fit the broad and diverse range of human experience. Moynihan declared "false" the theory "that you can run the nation from Washington . . . at least . . . with respect to the kind of social change liberals generally seek to bring about," which pertained to "social attitudes and practices."[44] Hence, we have the American system of federalism. "Federalism is not a managerial arrangement that the framers hit upon because the country was big and there were no telephones. . . . Federalism was a fundamental expression of the American idea of covenant."[45] In other words, federalism was about community. And community, to Moynihan, was fundamentally about diversity and pluralism—less diversity in the sense that we have come to attach to that word than in the sense of a multiplicity of units of social organization, both public and private, that would mediate between the individual and the larger society.

From this foundation arose Moynihan's devotion to the Catholic principle of subsidiarity, the idea that the state should not weaken social institutions close to the individual by removing from them superintendence over social problems they were competent to handle. Thus, for instance, a problem that could be resolved by the family should be so resolved in order to strengthen the family; similarly, something that could be handled by the neighborhood should be handled in that manner in order to strengthen the neighborhood. In several speeches and articles, Moynihan referred to Pius XI's encyclical *Quadragesimo Anno*, or *The Social Order*, which elucidated the principle of subsidiarity.[46] Pope John XXIII restated the centrality of subsidiarity in his 1961 *Mater et Magistra*. In a 1975 speech, Moynihan rued the fact that liberals who ought to have found so much affinity with the encyclical instead seemed to miss its point.

> Now a century earlier—just to keep matters complicated—such papal doctrine would have been seen as the embodiment of liberal principle! But by 1963 this was no longer so. To the contrary, American liberalism was at that very moment about to enter a period of unprecedented attachment to whatever it is that is the opposite of the principle of subsidiarity. The state was encouraged to take over more and more individual functions, and the highest levels of the state were encouraged to take over more and more of the functions of the "lesser and subordinate levels." There is every sign that American liberalism is just now coming out of this phase, and may indeed be adopting a principle of subsidiarity of its own.[47]

Several points are worthy of extended notice here. First, for Moynihan, classical liberalism and contemporary liberalism were continuous elements of the same tradition: a more or less straight line could be drawn from the classical liberalism of John Stuart Mill to the New Deal liberalism of Franklin Delano Roosevelt.[48] He described this evolution in more detail in his 1967 foreword to Alva Myrdal's *Nation and Family*: "Laissez-faire liberalism was concerned to liberate . . . all individuals from the interference of all institutions. . . . This tradition subtly transformed itself into the present-day concern to use the powers of the state to ease the impact on individuals of the more gross hazards of life."[49] Moynihan can reasonably be accused of appropriating the term *liberal* too loosely. The usage of the term had certainly evolved gradually (and unquestionably, it had indeed been applied first to Mill and eventually to Roosevelt), but arguably, it speciated along the way. Nonetheless, it is significant—and illuminating—that Moynihan sought to retain the connection, which reflects his simultaneous classical and contemporary liberal commitments.

Second and crucially, the date when subsidiarity was abandoned was 1963—the year of Kennedy's death and Johnson's ascension and the moment, for Moynihan, of transition between New Deal and Great Society liberalism. Most analysts would locate the deflection of liberalism from its nineteenth-century classical variant to its twentieth-century contemporary variant in the emergence of the Progressive movement. For Moynihan, however, it did not occur until the Great Society attempted not merely to ameliorate poverty but also to conquer it with programmatic efforts designed to micromanage the poor. The difference is comparable to Arthur Schlesinger's distinction between the "quantitative liberalism" of the New Deal, which sought to meet material needs, and the "qualitative liberalism" that the historian hoped would follow and assume a more transformative and forthright cast. Moynihan remained a partisan largely of the former variety.[50]

In Moynihan's view, the War on Poverty was different in kind from the New Deal. The New Deal was general and ameliorative, the War on Poverty micromanagerial and transformative.[51] Moynihan thought government competent to the first task but not the second. The War on Poverty, in fact, was quickly distorted into a vehicle for the interests of the professionals purportedly doing the transforming, so much so that he hypothesized the Great Society might actually have redistributed income upward by channeling money to middle-class service providers rather than the poor.[52] The distinction is evident in this reflection, which Moynihan wrote in the aftermath of the War on Poverty's disastrous "community action" programs: "Not long ago it could be agreed that politics was the business of who gets what, when, where, how. It is now more than that. It has become a process that also deliberately seeks to effect such outcomes as who *thinks* what, who *acts* when, who *lives* where, who *feels* how." He proceeded to claim that he did not "resist this development." But in reality, he *did* resist it—or at least rue it. Indeed, the passage is immediately followed with this observation: "That this description no more than defines a totalitarian society is obvious enough. But it has come to characterize democratic government as well."[53]

The New Deal was based on the principle of social insurance, the Great Society on service provision.[54] New Deal liberalism, which operated at the level of generality, ameliorated by taking wealth from one part of society and giving it to another. Great Society liberalism, by contrast, operated at the level of particularism—of individuals—by striving to transform or realign people's lives.[55] New Deal liberalism was sweeping in scope but simple in design; Great Society liberalism was composed of scattershot programs, invariably underfunded and uncoordinated. "The more programs, the less impact," Moynihan wrote, reflecting on the 1960s. And the Great Society certainly spawned a proliferation of programs.[56]

By redistributing wealth but remaining agnostic as to its use, New Deal liberalism left room for the intermediary institutions of a pluralistic society to flourish; Great Society liberalism was, by contrast, more statist in orientation. Thus, in *Family and Nation* (1985), Moynihan remarked that during the 1960s, "there was a division between new men with new enthusiasms—abolishing poverty, organizing communities, pursuing equality—and an older generation of New Dealers, men of the 1930s still pressing to complete a social insurance agenda."[57] In the book, he did not explicitly align himself with either camp, but it was clear where his sympathies lay, and it is especially interesting that he cast his implicit lot with amelioration over "equality." These sympathies were not entirely consistent. We have just, for example, encountered Moynihan's Democrats seeking change in "social attitudes and practices," which could hardly be quantified. But a clear tendency toward New Deal rather than Great Society liberalism, especially with respect to economic policy, continued to be evident in his work.

As will be discussed in chapter 2, this does not mean that Moynihan subscribed to the later-emergent narrative that the Great Society *caused* distress. On the contrary, he was often critical of its programs for being too small and underfunded, and his Moynihan Report of 1965 had charted data showing the indexes of despair at least in African American communities before the first shot in the War on Poverty was fired. The ~~int was that the approach of the Great Society as opposed to the New Deal failed—not a counsel of despair, again, but useful knowledge because it was reorienting. Throughout his life, Moynihan remained devoted to New Deal liberalism, but he became deeply skeptical of the Great Society variant as it pertained to welfare. Indeed, he wished that the Great Society had taken on simpler yet bolder goals: "The great failing of the Johnson administration was that an immense opportunity to institute more or less permanent social changes—a fixed full employment program, a measure of income maintenance—was lost."[58]

Finally, in his 1975 reflection on subsidiarity, decentralization emerged not merely as a principle of governance but also as one of ethics. To be clear, decentralization did not mean abandoning the role of the state. Instead, subsidiarity occupied a middle ground between the radical individualism that grew from classical liberalism and the statism that evolved from both continental socialism and conservative absolutists. The Anglo-American response was pluralism, the idea, Moynihan explained, "that between the individual and the state were to be found a great array of social and economic entities, and that in the strength of these voluntary, private associations—church, family, club, trade union, commercial association—lay much of the strength of democratic society."[59] But these institutions seemed inadequate to the depth of twentieth-century economic and military crises, leading nations to turn increasingly to the state to meet social needs.[60] This was not necessarily an unwelcome development in his view: "The result is an irreplaceable set of common provisions for the needy, the aged and the sick. But I sense that we are reaching a point at which it begins to be necessary to consider policies that will maintain a sound balance between our private and public spheres."[61]

Moynihan knew the importance of these subsidiary institutions. He was a product of them. It was not merely charm he intended to convey in relating an anecdote about his first experience with voting. In a 1987 speech, he recalled New York City's Hell's Kitchen neighborhood decades earlier:

> Families got in a fix. Boys got in a fix. Even, if the awful truth were known, girls, also. But neighborhoods were alright; there was a structure. (I can speak of this. I cast my first vote in 1948 in the basement of St. Raphael's at 10th Avenue and 42nd Street. I had been away in the Navy for three years and then college. I wasn't sure what to expect. I put on a tie and jacket. Entered. A man I'd never seen said: "Hi, Pat." I responded that I wasn't sure if I was eligible to vote. "Everybody votes," he replied, and as I entered the simple booth he handed me a palm card indicating who everybody was going to vote for.) That is to say there were imperfections in the arrangement, but it *was* an arrangement.[62]

The arrangement was strong neighborhoods. This lay at the root of Moynihan's concern as a senator that the Interstate Highway System had decimated cities, as well as his overhaul—one of his less appreciated but more enduring legislative achievements—of transportation policy to encourage experimentation with local needs such as mass transit.[63] And because strong neighborhoods also included strong institutions of religion, Moynihan long championed a proposal to allow parents to deduct the cost of parochial school tuition from their taxes. He argued that it would nourish institutions that helped educate the underprivileged, and he fiercely defended it against First Amendment challenges on the grounds that it did not constitute an establishment of religion.

This proposal provided the context for an address he delivered in 1979 at Fordham University, a Jesuit institution in New York City, just after the newly installed Pope John Paul II's visit to the United States. Moynihan began by referring to the pope's concern, expressed in his writings, with the problem of alienation; he noted, too, that the phenomenon, an essentially spiritual one, was also especially urban in character—clearing the path for the growth of the state at the expense of the civic sector. Moynihan stated, "A society suffused with the alienation of many of its members is a society that courts—if not totalitarianism, at least statism. The state thrives, prospers and grows in an atmosphere of alienation, for it is the only alternative to the purposeful, private, communal activity that decays in the presence of alienation."[64]

Supporters of Catholic institutions such as Fordham bore the responsibility, he said, "to find within the resources of liberal Catholic social thought the intellectual, moral and political capacity to defend" those values. Furthermore, American Catholic social thought might contribute to broader Catholic thought a deeper degree of comfort than the church had typically felt with private property and democratic capitalism as antidotes to statism. In particular, he asserted, "democratic capitalism" might provide "a non-socialist and non-statist alternative for providing for the common good," an alternative that mediated between individualism and community: "It suggests a means by which the principle Catholics call subsidiarity—the principle that social problems ought to be addressed by the social organism closest to them—can be and in the United States often is realized."

Subsidiary organizations "mediate[d] between the individual and the state . . . suggest[ing] an antidote to alienation, an end to anomie, and a curb on secular statism," he stated. To flourish, however, they required "a rather special environment that combines a free economy with free political institutions." Moynihan hinted several times at a gnawing fear that a reflexive advertence to the state eroded subsidiary institutions, much as Tocqueville warned that the transfer of once private functions to the state would leave the individual exposed to its power. This was not, however, an argument for laissez-faire. He proceeded to observe that "one of the finer achievements of American pluralism has been its demonstration that public policy can succor private institutions of every description"—apparently excepting, to his regret, institutions of religious education.

The state monopoly on education, he wrote elsewhere, manifested Schumpeter's "gloomy prophecy that liberalism will be destroyed through the steady conquest of the private sector by the public sector."[65]

During Senate debate on his bill, he remarked that the federal education bureaucracy "abhors that which it does not control. At the policy-making level, it is dominated by persons who have succumbed to a form of statism which they still, unaccountably, equate with liberalism."[66] Notice that subsidiarity was a liberal value, monopoly an antiliberal one. "Diversity. Pluralism. Variety. These are values, too, and perhaps nowhere more valuable than in the experiences that our children have in their early years, when their values and attitudes are formed, their minds awakened and their friendships formed."[67] Moynihan's point was not technocratic. Parochial schools were not better at education, but they educated *differently*. Moreover, they did so *privately*, and in the process, they mediated between the individual and the state, strengthened institutions of community, and thus mitigated the danger he often quoted from Emile Durkheim of society being reduced to a "dust of individuals."

The asserted state monopoly on education was symptomatic of the deeper ills of statism. He said in a 1978 speech: "We see increasing efforts to confer on public schools the presumption of exclusive legitimacy, and to regard private schools as if they existed at the sufferance of the state," even though private schools preceded public in the history of the Republic. The reason, he regretted, was that "the dominant symbols of liberalism in the late twentieth century are almost exclusively associated with activities carried out by the state."[68] Thus, in the 1979 speech to the United Way encountered in the introduction to this study—in which Moynihan delineated the difference between pluralist and statist liberalism—he questioned the claim of advocates of the latter strain that antitax and antigovernment sentiment reflected, in Senator George McGovern's words, a "degrading hedonism." The view was not "wholly wrong," but it was "disturbingly incomplete." One was not hedonistic simply by virtue of wanting to preserve a space for private institutions amid creeping statism. The challenge was for the voluntary sector to fill the space vacated by the state—but, crucially, government had a role to play in helping it do so. Moynihan wrote, "These [intermediate] institutions can be strengthened only when government and the 'third sector' cooperate to nurture them."[69]

One means of this nurturing involved his proposal to allow individuals who did not itemize deductions on their tax returns to deduct the cost of charitable contributions. He described its purpose in terms of subsidiarity. The national government should not assume responsibilities the states could carry out. It should not usurp communities, and communities, in turn, should preserve space for "the family itself, the neighborhood, the church," nonprofits, and the like. Subsidiarity, he noted, was the Catholic counterpart to federalism.[70]

Moynihan proceeded to consider the French Catholic philosopher Jacques Maritain's analysis in *Man and the State,* which argued against the "paternalist state."[71] According to Moynihan, the paternalist state appeared when the government assumed responsibility for activities that previously had been handled privately. However, he specified, many such activities were *properly* assumed by the public sphere in the modern era: "One cannot, for example, readily imagine cash assistance to the poor, the unemployed, the elderly and the disabled being provided as a matter of right other than by the state." The real problem was "the gradual submersion of private organizations that occurs as they become dependent on the state." Allowing individuals to deduct charitable contributions "above the line," he said, would "redress the balance a little. . . . It will restore a little more independence to the voluntary sector. It will add a bit to the ability of the ordinary working man or woman to determine how, and on what, some of his or her money is spent."[72] There would be some cost to public revenues, but "the alternative is gloomy indeed: A situation in which Government gradually assumes direct responsibility for practically everything and in which the generous impulses of philanthropists are snuffed out."[73]

Akin to this proposal was the one Moynihan offered much later in his Senate career to include a personal investment account as part of Social Security, which he described as a means not merely of preparing individuals for retirement but also of building a "property-owning democracy" that would lessen individuals' dependence on the state.[74] This would be a culminating innovation of American liberalism, which until then had copied its ideas on social insurance from European models. As he put it, "Americans [can] end their working lives with a measure of wealth. An estate. And for the first time, an American idea!"[75]

But no mediating force was more salient for Moynihan than the one that first put him on the scholarly map: ethnicity. His first book, cowritten with Nathan Glazer, was *Beyond the Melting Pot,* a study of the ethnic groups of New York City. It argued that contrary to the "liberal expectancy," which was the submergence of the supposed irrationality of ethnic attachments, such attachments persisted well past the massive European migration of the late nineteenth and early twentieth centuries. "The point about the melting pot," Glazer and Moynihan famously wrote, "is that it did not happen."[76] They found a rich array of ethnic affiliations that trumped social classes as means of identification. These, in turn, seemed to be a form of subsidiary institution for Moynihan, particularly insofar as they helped to organize local politics. However, ethnic identity was not without its costs. Moynihan reflected in 1977:

> Indeed, it was thought [by the liberal expectancy that] the sooner [ethnicity] disappeared the better. That, in our view, was not only to deny reality—a not very Madisonian prescription for the success of the Republic—but also to seek to strip something of true value from the lives of others. Our preference was unabashed: we approved St. Patrick's Day. The Feast of San Gennaro, Harlem, The Garment District, The Barrio. And yet I believe we sensed the potential for heartbreak in all this.[77]

The potential for heartbreak lay in the exploitation of ethnicity by both groups and the state. As Moynihan and Glazer had put it when they returned to the subject in a 1975 book, "The strategic efficacy of ethnicity as a basis for asserting claims against government has its counterpart in the seeming ease whereby government employs ethnic categories as a basis for distributing its rewards." The irony lay in the fact that this practice of government taking explicit cognizance of ethnicity arose immediately after the Civil Rights Act of 1964 prohibited precisely such practices.[78] Moynihan preferred strategies for racial equality that emphasized opportunities over quotas. He believed the society's failure to "assemble the political majority that would enable the nation to provide a free and equal place for the Negro in the larger society by what are essentially market strategies" would lead to coercive strategies "involving government-dictated outcomes directed against those institutions most vulnerable to government pressure. I don't like this mostly because I don't like that kind of government pressure." More significantly, "once this process gets legitimated there is no stopping it, and without intending anything of the sort, I fear it will be contributing significantly to the already well-developed tendency to politicize (and racialize) more and more aspects of modern life."[79]

This raised concerns about the efficacy of ethnicity as a subsidiary force, for it meant its co-optation by the state. "The general thrust of the modern state is to force all institutions to adopt its procedures and its objectives," he said in the 1977 speech. "No more the small platoons, beloved of Edmund Burke. Each unit of the society must be modeled on society itself. The result is the ever greater politicization of that society. I think we should resist this."[80] Yet the speech also suggests the pivotal uses Moynihan thought *could* be made of ethnicity. Its diversity preserved, it could create both mediating institutions and power structures that competed with the state. Such mediating institutions would mean the difference between statism, which he abhorred, and use of the state to attain social goals, which he embraced.

Moynihan's mixed feelings about ethnic attachment as a subsidiary force are also evident in his frank and, one is tempted to say, fearless talk about race, as a result of which he was pursued by charges of prejudice for years. In 1968, for instance, he wrote that "what the black community needs now is not excuses for its weakness, but encouragement to develop its strengths, and that means above all a turning away from violence."[81] But he also excoriated the War on Poverty for having excluded African Americans from its design and implementation.[82] He argued that what he called the color-blind social Darwinism of the Civil Rights Act of 1964 would not eventuate in equality because "racial inequality is imprinted in the very nerve system of American Society" through the medium of unequal education.[83] But his obvious sympathy for civil rights and equality of achievement did not insulate him from charges of racism when he advised President Nixon that "the issue of race could benefit from a period of 'benign neglect.'" Writing in a memo that "we may need a period in which Negro progress continues and racial rhetoric fades," Moynihan simply advised turning down the flame beneath the overheated *discussion* of the issue. But by the time the memorandum leaked, the story was that he had advised neglect of African Americans themselves.[84]

The principle of subsidiarity entered Moynihan's thought in a variety of ways beyond ethnicity. The community action programs of the War on Poverty, for example, reflected Nisbet's hollow "quest for community." Nisbet had written that as subsidiary institutions eroded, the need for institutions of community would persist, and individuals could consequently turn to the state to satisfy that need. Moynihan wrote: "The progress of secular liberalism had been one in which the institutions that formally mediated between the individual and the state had gradually eroded, as had relations between individuals. The result was anguished insecurity in the individual, and that in turn led, by a process of the politicization of personal anxiety, to totalitarianism in the state. Despotism, for being benevolent, was not thereby the less despotic."[85]

Nisbet had emphasized the consensual nature of authority and its distinction from the coercive character of power.[86] It was the former relationship that Moynihan saw collapsing in the erosion of the authority of civic institutions—authority that, he wrote in 1980, "has been grievously reduced in recent years." These institutions "formed slowly in America" but were collapsing suddenly.[87] The result was an "autonomous individual" who stood alone, exposed to the power of the state. In such an arrangement, that individual was responsible to the state, but responsibility did not run in the other direction. "Collectivism is not so far from the medieval concept of estate, with its notion of entitlement. *What is easily, and routinely, left out in the modern and secular version is the corresponding notion of obligation.*"[88] "Men," Moynihan concluded, "need a sense of community. . . . Burke[,] . . . Tocqueville, and Acton had in this respect at least been right. Not far removed would be the suggestion that on this point, the Catholic Church in much of its social teaching, had been right."[89]

Consequently, Moynihan generally strove to maintain a balance, sometimes elusive, between diffusing authority, on the one hand, and, on the other, national commitments on issues such as poverty. *"Liberals,"* he wrote, *"must divest themselves of the notion that the nation—and especially the cities of the nation—can be run from agencies in Washington."*[90] He traced what he called "Potomac Fever" to a turn-of-the-twentieth-century reformist assumption that local government was reactionary, so decision making should be elevated to the national level.[91] The inherent limits of bureaucracies now impelled decentralization. However, he added the decisive qualification: "To assert that government in Washington can't run everything is not to argue the impotence of government generally. Unfortunately, a good deal of decentralization talk is fundamentally antigovernment in spirit."[92]

Moynihan was dedicated to a broad array of subsidiary institutions. His resistance to statism and his commitment to mediating institutions explain his devotion to trade unionism. His political alliance with labor—which dated to his victory in the 1976 Democratic Senate primary in New York—reflected a commitment not just to the goals of that movement but also to its inherent utility as a buffer between the individual and the state. But no mediating institution was more important to him than the family. In a major civil rights address for President Johnson, he had written: "The family is the cornerstone of our society. More than any other force it shapes the attitudes, the hopes, the ambitions, and the values of the child. When the family collapses it is the children that are usually damaged. When it happens on a massive scale the community itself is crippled."[93]

Moynihan's attitude toward the family, which will be dealt with in more detail in chapter 2, was profoundly informed by Catholic social teaching. His 1985 Godkin Lectures at Harvard, published as *Family and Nation*, were committed to the idea that a coherent family policy could encourage family cohesion and, crucially, that welfare policy ought not to discourage it.

Here, however, we begin to touch the limits of government. A credible family policy will insist that responsibility begins with the individual, then the family, and only then the community, and in the first instance the smaller and nearer rather than the greater and more distant community. In papal encyclicals this is called "the principle of subsidiarity." Burke got it plainer when he talked of "the small platoons" of life. This is not a philosophical doctrine, it is a reality principle.[94]

Again referring to Burke, Moynihan wrote: "The decline in our social institutions is really without equivalent. Most importantly, and absolutely essential, is the decline of the family. The small platoons without which a society this large just cannot function."[95] As social institutions declined, government expanded to take their place, raising the illiberal danger of statism. He thus worried about the absolute growth in the size of government during the late 1960s and 1970s, which was on target to reach 50 percent of the economy by the end of the twentieth century, a circumstance he feared would be unrecognizable. Notice, however, that this was, for Moynihan, an essentially liberal rather than conservative concern; put otherwise, he worried as a liberal, not as a conservative. The particular worry pertained to pluralism. As government grew, "the more then is the importance of those institutions of the culture . . . which remain private. If there is a single task with which liberalism in the large sense of that word ought to be concerned in the period ahead, it is with the well-being and prosperity of such private institutions." The "size of the central establishment" was both a "conservative" *and* a "liberal" concern, one to be redressed partly through the mechanism of federalism.[96]

Again, though, this was not an antigovernment counsel. In fact, enhancing the voluntary sector might also have strengthened the public one. "I am prepared to believe," he declared, "that the two can prosper alongside one another, indeed, that neither can serve us well without the other. Tocqueville understood this, as he did so many things."[97] The particular difficulty, as Moynihan wrote in an extensive paper for Nelson Rockefeller's Bicentennial Commission on Critical Choices for Americans, was that Americans displayed a split personality on the topic of government's size, agitating for less while choosing more: "The modern state has surprisingly similar effects on the individual as it moves from minimal concern to total involvement. The critical choice is not what it does, but how much it does."[98] By the time of the Reagan era deficits, he "detect[ed] a measure of dissembling, if not contradiction, in our well-known aversion to Big Government. . . . It was clear enough that individuals and groups had considerable tolerance for government outlays that benefited them."[99] The Reagan administration's structural slashing of revenues, which was supposed to be but was not followed by an equally steep cut in spending, supplied a test that the public failed. Historically, Americans' devotion to fiscal responsibility was "a kind of civic religion, avowed but not constraining."[100] Conversely, just as maintaining the voluntary sector might help strengthen the public one, Moynihan argued the public sector could help to nourish the voluntary one—although the precise dimensions of this policy approach were less clear.

ASPIRATIONS

We have seen, then, that Moynihan prized limitation and appreciated social complexity. These are the Burkean strains in his thought. But he was, again, a liberal, and so we come now to the particular character of Moynihan's liberalism, for a portrait centered solely on his admiration for the voluntary and private sectors would be entirely incomplete. The essence of his liberalism lay in his belief in government as an agent of amelioration and progress. In a 1967 address, he defined liberalism's "essentials" as consisting of "an optimistic belief in progress, in toleration, in equality, in the rule of law, and in the possibility of attaining a high and sustained measure of human happiness here on earth."[101] This should be

distinguished from "progressivism," at least as it is theoretically understood—that is, as an inherent faith in progress. The distinction involves
the *possibility* of progress as opposed to its *inevitability*. Moynihan observed in a 1969 lecture that "the idea of a society confidently directed to
ever higher levels of social justice and equality has been shaken by the
obstinacy of things."[102] Nonetheless, he believed a high and sustained
measure of happiness was possible, just not inevitable.

Government played an indispensable role in enabling that happiness
insofar as material prosperity was a precondition for it but, significantly,
not by micromanaging the terms of its delivery. This emerged as a decisive difference between New Deal and Great Society liberalism, the former assuming an ameliorative and the latter a transformative cast. "The
federal government is good at collecting revenues, and rather bad at dis-
bursing services," Moynihan observed. "Therefore, we should use the
Federal fisc as an instrument for redistributing income between different levels of government, different regions and different classes."[103]
Family allowances—payments to families based on the number of children they had—were a vehicle "for redistributing income in such a way
as to benefit the child-rearing portion of a nation's population"; further,
this approach recognized that the wage system did not respond to the
variable of family size.[104] Crucially, Moynihan contended, government
succeeded when it acted in this manner: "The American national government is a superb instrument for redistributing power and wealth in
our society. One person in ten in the United States, for example, now
gets a Social Security check every month."[105] The result was that poverty
among the elderly had been dramatically reduced.

Moreover, government was to be, as we have seen, an "instrument of
common purpose." For this reason, Moynihan particularly objected to
the early Reagan administration's claim that it no longer intended to
utilize the tax code to achieve "social change." He replied that this was
impossible. The manner of extracting taxes from society inevitably
shaped society; the question was merely how. "There . . . is the difference
that divides Democrats from Republicans. . . . To say that taxes must not
be used to bring about social change," he argued, "is to say there should

be no public schools. No public hospitals. No system of social welfare. No public housing. No public beaches. No public television."[106] As a self-described political thinker of the "liberal center," Moynihan recognized the essential role of the private sector, both in terms of pluralism and as an agent of producing the wealth he wanted government to redistribute. He objected, for example, to the "radical disjunction" in liberal thought "between the production of wealth and its distribution, with the accompanying view that the former takes care of itself and that the task of government is to see to the latter."[107] Paraphrasing the economist Charles Schultze, he observed the tendency of government to respond to problems in the private sector not by restructuring private incentives but rather by transferring power from the private to the public sector, resulting in "social interventions that are staggeringly complex, and ultimately futile. Save, I would add, that in the end government commences to be satisfied with whatever increases its power, however little it may increase its efficacy."[108] But from that position in the center, Moynihan celebrated "the activist national liberalism of the New Deal. I am unabashedly a product of that tradition. It incorporates an ethic of collective provision. . . . We are a vastly stronger, more united, and happier nation thanks to Franklin D. Roosevelt and the ideas he stood for."[109]

The redistribution of wealth was not the only lever available to the political sector to improve society. It could, as Moynihan suggested in the epigraph to this chapter, go so far as to "change a culture and save it from itself." In many ways, this was a stunning statement of the capacities of government for someone so aware of its limitations. But the key to understanding it may lie in the sentence often omitted from the quotation, in which Moynihan selected an illustration of a culture that required "saving from itself": "Witness the civil rights legislation of the 1960s that conservatives so opposed."[110] Things that government was naturally supposed to do—and surely enforcing civil rights was among them—could also transform attitudes. Family policy was another such area. It was not necessary for government to set out on a utopian course to reshape the culture; it only had to seek out points of contact at which attitudes and practices could respond to public actions and incentives.

These, for Moynihan, were myriad. In the case of civil rights, the government had activated those touch points and succeeded:

> The middle third of the twentieth century in the United States was, for all its ambiguities, a period of extraordinary social idealism and not less extraordinary social progress. . . . The nation entered this period bound to the mores of caste and class. The white race was dominant. . . . In a bare third of a century these circumstances have been extensively changed. *Changed!* Not merely a sequence of events drifting in one direction or another. To the contrary, events have been bent to the national will. Things declared to be desirable have been attained through sustained and systematic effort.[111]

The bold readiness to undertake such efforts was one factor dividing liberals from conservatives and one perhaps dividing, in points of emphasis, Moynihan the statesman from Moynihan the scholar. Liberals pursued a guaranteed income during the Nixon administration despite being unable firmly to forecast its consequences—a staple reservation of conservative thought. "Political liberals were willing nonetheless to take the chance, indeed were anxious to if only for the excitement of it all," Moynihan reported.[112] And in a 1985 paper, he discussed the twin roles of scholar and statesman—the caution of the former but the latter's need for action—writing that "government is going to have to be involved" in social policy. "But I would offer the thought," he continued, "that there are huge areas of social policy of which it must be said that today either we don't know what to do or don't know how to do it." The character of his liberalism is revealed in his response to that ignorance, which was not caution but rather what might be characterized as boldness within boundaries: "This is a true and worthy challenge. We need a rebirth of social policy as both a moral and an empirical exercise, free of the mindless millennialism of the past and the equally thoughtless meanness of the present."[113] This optimism was bounded, as we have seen, by a sense of limitation not merely as a condition of politics but also as a condition of life.

Even while acknowledging the shortcomings of the Great Society, he was eager in the Reagan years for his Democratic Party to recover its self-confidence. "The Copperhead Democrats of the Civil War never repented," he observed. "The veterans and inheritors of the New Deal and the Great Society do little else."[114] Nonetheless, early in *The Politics of a Guaranteed Income,* Moynihan's analysis of the collapse of his proposal for family allowances, he declared with confidence, "I write in praise of democratic government. . . . I propound no notion of systemic genius which spares us the fate of less fortunate people. I only state that my experience of American government is that it is a decent process, and commands my regard."[115] His volume of Reagan era essays and speeches, published as *Came the Revolution: Argument in the Reagan Era,* was originally entitled *In Defense of Government.*[116] In it, he counseled Democrats: "The one sure thing is to learn to use our heads again. By all means let us go on about self-reliance, gumption, and go gettingness. Nothing the matter with any of the above. But if that is all there is to be by way of social policy, no one needs Democrats. And if that is all the social policy there is to be, Democrats shall have deserved their eclipse."[117]

Social policy, then, was uniquely associated with liberalism, and he consistently applied the liberal label to himself. In one rousing political speech in early 1981, he declared:

> Four years and some months ago on the evening I was elected to the Senate, I said on television that "I ran as a liberal. I was elected as a liberal." I say to you tonight that I have served as a liberal and I will continue to do so. For I am a Democrat of New York County. Coming home from World War II, I cast my first vote in St. Raphael's Church on 41st and 10th Avenue in Hell's Kitchen. And I will face Hell itself before I go back on that tradition.[118]

What, then, should we make of Moynihan's frequent criticisms of liberalism and liberals? The answer is that these were criticisms borne of love. His motive was regard for the liberal tradition, not disillusionment and certainly not contempt. Of his criticism of the War on Poverty, he wrote that liberalism "can respond to criticism from within, and needs that criticism as much now as ever."[119] In 1976, during his first campaign for the Senate, he said: "I ran as a liberal willing to be critical of what liberals had done. If we did not do this, I contended, our liberalism would go soft."[120] Democrats would emerge more robust from a vigorous struggle with Republicans, having been forced to shed their gradually accreted identity as the "Party of Government."[121] In a speech to Democrats in California in 1978, Moynihan quoted Lionel Trilling on the need for "opponents who will do us the service of forcing us to become more intelligent, who will require us to keep our ideas from becoming stale and inert." Notice how Moynihan understood his own task: "As one who has tried to do this in what is now a quarter century of party work . . . I can attest that it has not always been an agreeable task, but at least it has been an easier one than facing serious external challenge."[122]

His liberalism also resisted the radicalization of the 1960s because of his insistence on regularity and restraint. He again classified as liberal such values as respect for "human frailty":

> The less than soul-stirring belief of the liberal in due process, in restraint, in the rule of law is something more than a bourgeois *apparat*: it involves, I argue, the most profound perception of the nature of human society that has yet been achieved, and, precisely in its acknowledgment of the frailty of man and the persistence of sin and failure, it is in the deepest harmony with the central tradition of Judeo-Christian theology. It is not a belief to be frittered away in deference to a mystique of youth.[123]

In theological terms, this is fundamentally a philosophy of man's fall and thus of human limitation—another sense in which Moynihan's Catholicism was both evident in his political thought and essentially conducive to a Burkean disposition. That he described it as liberal underscores his association of that tradition with limitation and his rejection of attempts, under its flag, at projects of human perfectibility.

Moynihan lamented the inability of liberals, "trapped in their own decencies," to confront squarely the emergent problem of an urban underclass.[124] His sympathy for these liberals was genuine; so, however, was his contempt for the shallow radicalism that came to dominate left-wing discourse in the 1960s. He noted that the Port Huron Statement, the 1962 manifesto of student activists, barely mentioned such problems as poverty: "It is addressed exclusively to middle class intellectuals and college students."[125] He diagnosed this "youthful protest" as arising from anomie driven by the rationalism of the "educated elite," which caused "the wellsprings of emotion [to] dry up, and in particular the primal sense of community [to begin] to fade."[126] But his understanding of the phenomenon did not excuse its excesses. He expressed "a considerable contempt both for those who threaten violence and those who countenance it." He rejected "the great debasement of language and the fantasizing of politics that accompanied the reaction" to Vietnam.[127] This form of protest became the plaything of privilege: "The president of Yale toyed with it; the president of the AFL-CIO wouldn't touch it."[128]

NEOCONSERVATISM

The degree to which Moynihan felt politics could play a constructive role in attaining his optimistic vision separates him from a tradition—what its godfather Irving Kristol called an "impulse"—with which he has frequently been linked: neoconservatism.[129] We shall encounter the breaks between Moynihan and neoconservatives in subsequent chapters as areas of his thought are explored in more detail, especially foreign policy, but a brief sketch is in order here. The term *neoconservatism* generally has referred to a strain of conservatism derived from disillusioned former liberals typified by Kristol—liberals, in his formulation, who had been "mugged by reality." Moynihan would refer to the period of their disillusionment as liberalism's "Reformation": "Not a few of the heretics were burned at the stake, and more than a few left the true church for good and all."[130] But despite his heretical disposition and his lifelong friendships with those who left the faith, Moynihan was not among them. He wrote at the beginning of the Reagan administration, "I was by this time a bit estranged from a greatly gifted circle of New York writers who first came together in dismay at the 'liberal' politics of the 1960s. Many had gone over to the Republicans: many had entered the new administration or assertively supported it. I hadn't, didn't, wouldn't, don't."[131]

Moynihan has nonetheless been associated with neoconservatives for a variety of reasons, not least because he kept company with many of them in both print and his personal life, counting writers such as Kristol and Norman Podhoretz among his closest friends and journals such as *Commentary* and *Public Interest* among his favorite places to publish. His beliefs, especially his antitotalitarianism, overlapped with theirs in key respects. His criticism of the Great Society could be seen to correspond with criticisms they leveled as well.

But fissures begin to open on close examination. Kristol's eight-point manifesto for neoconservatism held that a "conservative welfare state—what once was called a 'social insurance' state—is perfectly compatible with the neoconservative perspective."[132] The precise contours of this welfare state are unclear; what is clear is that Moynihan would have sought more than mere "compatibility" between his beliefs and a national commitment to welfare. He was a forthright supporter of such a program throughout his career. The extent of its generosity would split Moynihan from the neoconservatives and their successors, many of whom were disappointed by his crusade against the repeal of the national guarantee of welfare benefits in 1995 and 1996. Furthermore, unlike the subsequent generation of those who donned the neoconservative mantle, Moynihan's commitment to a foreign policy that stood for human rights was never expansionist or expeditionary. And finally, there is the fact that Moynihan so fiercely resisted the neoconservative label.

We may ask, of course, what is in a name—especially if his beliefs corresponded with Kristol's in several particulars—but the fact that Moynihan thought there was so much, as well as such perniciousness, in this particular label illuminates the extent of his liberalism. He often said he told his students that the most significant datum in registering a person's political beliefs was when he or she was born. Moynihan thus wrote to a *New York Times* reporter in one of several attempts to disassociate himself from the neoconservative label: "My 'ideological roots' are not, and in truth could not be, in the 'neo-conservative movement.' I am a 56 year old man: my ideological roots are in the Democratic party of Franklin D. Roosevelt."[133]

THE POLITICS OF PUBLIC PLACES

Moynihan's faith in government also found expression in his lifelong advocacy of a confident and forthright style of public architecture. He often quoted Thomas Jefferson's remark that "design activity and political thought are indivisible."[134] Architecture was "the one inescapably public art, which is no more than to say, that government can have as little involvement with the arts generally as it chooses, save that it cannot avoid architecture." In turn, architecture "reports faithfully for ages to come what the political values of a particular era were."[135] Conveying those values was one of the greatest and most consistent passions of Moynihan's career. Among his duties in the Kennedy administration that would have the most lasting impact was the drafting of what remain to this day the "Guiding Principles of Federal Architecture," which called for "an architectural style and form which is distinguished and which will reflect the dignity, enterprise, vigor, and stability of the American National Government."[136]

Moynihan regretted that "somehow, somewhere, in the course of the development of democratic or demagogic tradition in this nation, the idea arose that concern with the physical beauty of the public buildings and spaces of this city and nation was the mark of mistaken priorities." Consequently, he argued, the quality of public buildings and spaces had eroded, "and with it [came] a decline in the symbols of public unity and common purpose with which the citizen can identify, of which he can be proud, and by which he can know what he shares with his fellow citizens."[137] The sense of community and common purpose that Moynihan saw as central to government wore away as a result. And so, too, did the quality of government: "Men who build bad buildings are bad governors," and "a people that persists in electing such men is opting for bad government."[138]

No passion was more enduring for Moynihan than his leadership of the effort to restore Washington's Pennsylvania Avenue. As of the early Kennedy administration, the stretch connecting the Capitol with the White House was a dilapidated expanse of slums and abandoned buildings. Moynihan took his cue from Pierre L'Enfant, the architect of Washington, D.C., who had designed the city with political principles in mind, laying out "a kind of diagram of the Constitution" with Congress at the center, separated from the president yet connected, too. "This was to be a new kind of government," Moynihan said, "and its arrangement had to be made clear. This is what the Avenue does."[139] To the extent the restoration project succeeded, he believed it was because of "a certain political literacy which we brought to the enterprise, a sense of the possibilities of the future that can only be acquired by an informed study and concern for the past."[140]

It was particularly important to Moynihan to avoid a Stalinoid architecture of enormity, a concern that took hold as it became clear Pennsylvania Avenue would be "lined on either side with government buildings." He criticized the "architecture of coercion" that Governor Nelson Rockefeller of New York imposed in Albany: "Man, in the Presence of the State, Thou Art Nothing. This is what we wanted to prevent [on Pennsylvania Avenue], and we did."[141] "Magnificence," he reflected on another occasion, "does not mean monumentality."[142]

This restoration of public spaces was integral to Moynihan's understanding of politics as a common endeavor rooted, most significantly, in a common past. Architecture could help to recapture that past. Symbols mattered. Subsidiarity echoes in his reflection on "shared experience" and "trust":

> If we are to save our cities and restore to American public life the
> sense of shared experience, trust, and common purpose that seems

to be draining out of it, the quality of public design has got to be made a public issue because it *is* a political fact. The retreat from magnificence, to use a phrase of Evelyn Waugh's, has gone on long enough: too long. An era of great public works is as much needed in America as any other single element in our public life.[143]

What the nation chose to conserve could be as critical as what it chose to build, for common memory was a spur to common action. Moynihan said in the Senate in 1983, "We must not preserve buildings out of a fear that we have lost the ability to create things of grace and beauty. . . . I wish to preserve things as an example of what we were and will be, not what we were and no longer can be."[144]

MOYNIHAN'S CONSTITUTION

L'Enfant's Washington placed Congress at the center. So, during his service in the Senate, did Moynihan's Constitution. To be sure, he clearly believed in the need for a strong presidency. He viewed Nixon's fall as a tragedy; reacted to Reagan's near collapse over the Iran contra affair with alarm; and responded to Clinton's impeachment, despite his thinly veiled contempt for the president's behavior, with reserve. Yet a strong presidency did not mean either a royal or a lawless one. Moynihan opposed the inflation of the Secret Service into a "protective service grown to the size and sometimes the pretension of a praetorian guard." Not even Woodrow Wilson, he suggested, would recognize the contemporary presidency: "A president who wrote and typed his own speeches is now at some removes succeeded by presidents who do not know the names of most of their speechwriters, much less of their lawyers, economists, statisticians, strategists, and yes, as of 1989 the White House demographer. First the president got staff, then the staff got staff."[145]

The presidency was nearly consumed when Congress cut off aid to the Nicaraguan contras and the Reagan administration decided to seek what Moynihan characterized as "third-country funding." He wrote that

Reagan "invite[d] and almost certainly did deserve impeachment" for the perversion of the Constitution that resulted.[146] But Moynihan's regard for the office of the presidency and his view of its centrality to the constitutional order were such that he resisted imposing this ultimate punishment. On the weekend after the Iran contra story broke, Democrats chose Moynihan to deliver their response to Reagan's radio address. In it, he fairly pleaded with the chief executive:

> Your Presidency, sir, is tottering. It can be saved. But only you can save it, and only if you will talk to us, the Congress. . . . Men have betrayed your trust. Very well, let it all come out in the open with greater than deliberate speed, immediately, regardless. And so I plead, Mr. President, clean house. Out with all the facts. Out with all the malefactors. Come to the Hill and talk, elected official to elected official. We are your friends. We share this brief but sacred authority given us by the American people. We want you to save your presidency, our presidency.[147]

Moynihan's tolerance, however, was limited. When the Tower Commission, which investigated the Iran contra scandal, issued a report calling the administration's conduct an "aberration," Moynihan retorted that "it was nothing of the sort. It was part of a persistent pattern of illegality and irresponsibility." Legislation was not needed; legislation was already in place: "It didn't work because the people didn't believe in the legislation. That's called law-breaking. . . . It's not a problem of management style. It's a fundamentally flawed view of the American government."[148] Moynihan's reaction to the Iran contra affair reflected the adamant defense of congressional and particularly Senate prerogatives he maintained throughout his career. As early as 1966, fresh from his tenure in the executive branch, Moynihan was already aware of an imbalance in knowledge between the White House and Congress, and he proposed that it be redressed by the latter establishing a research arm that he dubbed the Office of Legislative Evaluation.[149] As a senator, he fiercely opposed both the Gramm-Rudman-Hollings Act—which would have triggered automatic spending cuts if Congress failed to enact them—and the line-item veto as abdications of congressional authority and, crucially, responsibility. When the Supreme Court declared Gramm-Rudman-Hollings unconstitutional, Moynihan said "the shame [was] that the Court had to force Congress to face its constitutional duty—a responsibility to choose that we never should have relinquished in the first place."[150] In a subsequent floor speech, he addressed the issue as one of congressional versus presidential authority: "We have no constitutional therapy for this abdication of responsibility. The Constitution gives this Congress the responsibility to make up a budget to raise the ways and means to provide for government, and it does not allow it to abdicate that responsibility and ask some father figure in the White House to do it for them. No. Adults dreamed up this Constitution and adults will have to preserve it."[151]

The line-item veto, he argued, could not be imposed legislatively and would, moreover, alter the balance of power between the legislative and executive branches. "Mr. President," he began a Senate address as the bill neared a vote, "I rise in the serene confidence that this measure is constitutionally doomed."[152] Among other problems, the line-item veto would upset the fragile balance of compromises that any complex bill represented, but it would also give presidents an additional means of subtle coercion to use in their dealings with members of Congress.[153] As a result, both Gramm-Rudman-Hollings and the line-item veto would have disrupted what Moynihan saw as the sine qua non of the constitutional regime—the separation of powers. He noted that the separation of powers built the mechanism of competition into the political order, calling it "the central principle of the Constitution."[154] The essence of the Founders' "new science of politics"—their core innovation in the history of political thought—was to presume conflict rather than harmony.[155] He drew deeply on such sources as *The Federalist* to back these reflections, as he did in quoting James Madison's dictum that men were not angels. "Not pretty," Moynihan noted, "but something far more important: predictable."[156]

His most sustained and deepest reflection on the Constitution and its political theory occurred during a long Senate speech defending the Electoral College that he delivered in 1979. Moynihan recalled an afternoon of boredom in the General Assembly of the United Nations during his ambassadorship, during which he looked at the two large voting boards that listed the names of member nations. "I found myself asking how many of the 143—now 154—nation member[s] of the U.N. had existed in 1914 and had not had their governments changed by force since 1914. . . . Exactly seven met both those criteria. . . . In no small measure [US success] has been the result of the genius of the American Constitution and the way it has served this political community for almost two centuries."[157]

The Founders, he said, citing the political scientist Martin Diamond, believed liberty was a "primary political good" whose value could be ascertained through reason and secured through discoveries made possible by the "new science of politics." One of those was the principle that John C. Calhoun called "concurrent majorities."[158] "All through our system we find majorities at work," Moynihan said by way of defending the Electoral College against a proposed constitutional amendment to replace it with direct election of the president, "but they have to be at work simultaneously." Concurrent majorities operated in the requirement that a bill command majorities of the people through the House and the states through the Senate; between the majorities in Congress who pass a bill and the president who signs it; and, vitally, between the combination of majorities, those of the people and of the states, required to elect that president in the first place.

The "principle of the electoral college," he stated, was "the need to see that power is never installed, save when it is consented to by more than one majority." This, in turn, reflected the theoretical innovation of building conflict into the constitutional regime: "There is no prior existence anywhere, even in the ancient constitutions of the Greeks, which recognized that conflict was normal to a political system and needed to be organized and channeled. . . . James Madison knew better. He knew conflict was normal or perpetual. He believed that it could be controlled."

One device that emerged for the channeling of conflict was the political party.[159] Because the Electoral College required majorities to moderate themselves, parties had proven to be moderate, too. American parties "had as their single most characteristic quality—again, different from anything else in the experience of republics—that they were not ideological, that they were not sectional nor confessional, and never, in the two great parties, extreme." The Electoral College made it impossible for them to be so "if they [were] to continue effectively to be parties."

The abolition of the Electoral College, he warned, would alleviate the pressure for consensus. "If we would study the modern history of Europe as [the Founders] studied the ancient history of Greece, what would we repeatedly encounter but a democratic-republican society succumbing to a plebiscitory majority and to one man and to the end of the republic?" he asked. Parties facing the pressure to build electoral majorities, by contrast, would seek "very little that is inspiring to youth and much that is consoling to the aged, to wit, a not always pristine consensus."

Respect for judicial independence also played a central role in Moynihan's constitutional politics. Richard K. Eaton reflected that Moynihan became "something of a protector of what Alexander Hamilton called 'the least dangerous branch' because he [knew] that by custom it is unable to speak for itself."[160] He consequently responded with grave concern to attempts to use Congress's constitutional authority to strip the federal courts of jurisdiction over cases when legislators were unhappy with their rulings. The American Bar Association had somewhat hyperbolically called this "the greatest constitutional crisis since the Civil War," a phrase Moynihan borrowed. Rather than trying to persuade the Supreme Court of its errors—a model Moynihan cast as "debate, litigate, legislate"—Republicans in Congress, outraged by the federal courts' busing orders for public schools, had substituted a model of convene (propose a constitutional convention to reverse adverse court rulings), overturn (reverse them through ordinary legislation), and restrict (limit the jurisdiction of certain courts to decide certain cases). Although the last of these was "colorably constitutional," Moynihan observed, it was also "profoundly at odds with our nation's customs and political philosophy. It is a commonplace that our democracy is characterized by majority rule and minority rights. Our Constitution vests majority rule in the Congress and the President while the courts protect the rights of the minority."[161] Accordingly, he unsuccessfully offered a constitutional amendment to prevent Congress from stripping the Supreme Court's jurisdiction over constitutional cases.[162]

On several occasions, Moynihan warned against tampering with the protections of the Bill of Rights, often swimming against strong political tides to do so. In the aftermath of the Oklahoma City bombing, he spoke against the Terrorism Prevention Act of 1995, which limited habeas corpus petitions in federal courts: "If I had to choose between living in a country with habeas corpus but without free elections, or a country with free elections but without habeas corpus, I would choose habeas corpus every time."[163] In a 1995 interview, he raised a concern about civil liberties, but note the Burkean overtones in his dismissal of libertarianism: "If we had a Constitutional Convention these days, which the Constitution makes possible, you wouldn't get much of the Bill of Rights in it. And, that is a mark of a society more fearful of liberty than we have been in the past, because liberty has become libertarian. It has lost its contact with responsibility, with restraint, with measured judgments. What's that?"[164]

He would later oppose the Victim's Rights Amendment to the Constitution, pronouncing himself appalled by the casualness with which it was considered in the Senate—where debate on this occasion proceeded with virtually no senators present. "The capacity of American culture in this stage to think of new forms of victimhood is unprecedented," he remarked. "It has been a characteristic of the culture for a generation now to declare oneself a victim and demand compensation and consideration." By way of warning, Moynihan recalled the joke that librarians file the French constitution under "Periodicals." "We have a treasure here," he said, "the oldest written Constitution on Earth. . . . If we are to trivialize the Constitution, we risk its stability."[165]

"THE FIRST RESPONSIBILITY OF LIBERALISM"

Moynihan believed that democratic governance was conducted through words and that liberals had a particular responsibility to preserve the integrity of language. As early as 1964, he would hail the War on Poverty for calling "a particularly ugly fact by its rightful name."[166] In a 1972 article, he lamented the "upper-class lying" that was "destroying the standards of discourse": "The language of politics grows more corrupt. . . . We are beginning to encounter middle-of-the-road politicians who will seemingly say anything. We approach a fantasized condition."[167] At the height of the Cold War, he feared that "the West's political culture is endangered by the fact that the vocabulary and the symbols of political progress are being expropriated by the opponents of our values."[168] By 1996, as the Clinton administration and congressional Republicans joined forces to end Aid to Families with Dependent Children, he would complain bitterly about the "monstrous political deception embodied in the term 'welfare reform.' In my lifetime there has been no such Orwellian inversion of truth in the course of a domestic debate. 'Welfare reform' in fact means welfare repeal."[169]

Moynihan never more stridently or compellingly defended the integrity of language than during his crusade against the notorious "Zionism is racism" resolution at the United Nations in 1975, a story he retold in *A Dangerous Place*. He understood himself to be defending words as the currency of political exchange, and he cast this as a liberal task: "I had wanted to speak to the issue of language; to say that to preserve the meaning of words is the first responsibility of liberalism."[170] In his famous speech denouncing the resolution, he declared: "What we have here is a lie—a political lie of a variety well known to the twentieth century, and scarcely exceeded in all that annal of untruth and outrage. The lie is that Zionism is a form of racism. The overwhelmingly clear truth is that it is not." In somewhat professorial style, he proceeded to explain the impossibility of understanding Zionism to be racism because, among other factors, one could convert to Judaism but could not choose one's race. His broader point addressed the danger of perverting the meaning of words:

> Today we have drained the word "racism" of its meaning.
> Tomorrow, terms like "national self-determination" and "national honor" will be perverted in the same way to serve the purposes of conquest and exploitation. And when these claims begin to be made—as they already have begun to be made—it is the small nations of the world whose integrity will suffer. And how will the small nations of the world defend themselves, on what grounds will others be moved to defend and protect them, when the language of human rights, the only language by which the small can be defended, is no longer believed and no longer has a power of its own? . . . There is this danger, and then a final danger that is the most serious of all. Which is that the damage we now do to the idea of human rights and the language of human rights could well be irreversible.[171]

Language, so conceived, constituted a form of limitation in itself. It confined political discourse. Words had meanings. The business of politics was to be conducted through them; they could not merely be inflated to mean whatever it was convenient to the speaker or listener for them to mean. But words also encapsulated the sense of shared possibilities that politics enabled—in this case, the aspiration of human rights, whose meaningful promise was precisely why words such as *racism* should *not* be drained of meaning. And there we have, in brief, the two central truths that frame Moynihan's thought and whose intertwining renders its contours so unique.

One is the liberal belief in the possibilities that could be animated by the shared enterprise of politics. The second is the traditionally conservative belief—although Moynihan classified it, as we have seen, as liberal—in the limitations of human action, especially where complex systems such as the social organism were concerned. It would oversimplify Moynihan's thought to say the second of these beliefs merely acted as a brake on the first. Instead, the two were engaged in an intricate dance, with limits helping to identify possibilities and possibilities bound by limits. With that understanding in place, we may now see how this blend—what I have called Burkean liberalism—played out in Moynihan's thought.

2. Poverty and Problems
Poorly Stated

The American welfare system is one of the proudest achievements of a generous and compassionate people. But it must not be allowed to become the economic system of a permanent sub-culture. Men need jobs, families need fathers, communities need independence. This must be our objective, and it is an objective entirely compatible with the fullest care for those individuals who find themselves temporarily or even permanently unable to look after themselves.

—Moynihan, *Enterprise,* October 1964

Those involved will take this disgrace to their graves. The children alone are innocent.

—Moynihan, House-Senate conference on welfare reform, 1995

Moynihan knew—knew nearly from the moment the first shot in the War on Poverty was fired—that the battle would be lost, but not for the reasons commonly supposed. He has often been associated with the conservative trope that the generosity of Great Society programs induced social pathologies such as welfare dependency and family dissolution among the poor. In fact, however, his criticism came from the opposite direction: he argued that the War on Poverty was waged with inadequate vigor. He believed the government failed to spend enough money on the poor and, crucially, to spend it directly on them. Instead, the Johnson administration opted for a "services" strategy that Moynihan, with characteristic incisiveness, suggested might have redistributed income upward from poor taxpayers to middle-class social workers. Since poverty was an experience of material privation, what poor people needed most of all was money, and he believed the national government should provide it, especially for children. This belief in a national commitment, particularly to children, runs throughout Moynihan's career-long journey through poverty policy, which otherwise winds through changing evidence and circumstances. But Moynihan rejected the thesis that the Great Society caused social pathologies, noting they were evident even before the War on Poverty began and that they were rising in all nations of the Atlantic world, regardless of their welfare policies.

The issue of poverty assumed deeply moral and also religious dimensions for Moynihan. In a reflective address before the National Council of Churches in 1964, he wondered why a Christian "should not seek to embrace poverty rather than seek to eliminate it." Christ, after all, had done the former. The reason to eliminate it, he explained, was that—unlike the poverty of biblical experience, which enabled Christ to forge a connection with the common experience of the vast majority of people—contemporary poverty was divisive, causing the poor to be "excluded from the great company of our society."[1] He frequently invoked Pope John XXIII's encyclical *Mater et Magistra*, which declared a "right" of labor. "Right, repeat, right," Moynihan emphasized: "In an industrial world that has not yet come to terms with the question of leisure, men without work are deprived of an essential condition of human dignity."[2]

He was especially and consistently concerned about childhood poverty, noting that America was tragically exceptional in becoming "the first society in history in which the poorest group in the population were children."[3] He called attention to the striking contrast between the nation's success in substantially reducing poverty among the elderly and its seeming indifference to the same phenomenon among the young, as well as politicians' occasional proclivity to redistribute resources from impoverished families with children to the comparatively well-off aged.[4] He believed the welfare reform of 1996, which replaced national guarantees of benefits to the poor with block grants to states while imposing a five-year lifetime limit on aid, was a morally deplorable risk—above all because it gambled with the lives of children, revoking a decades-old federal commitment to their well-being. This was an issue of principle for Moynihan, and he felt strongly that the Clinton White House, which supported the bill, should be "ashamed" that it was willing to take the risk merely to promote the president's reelection even though an administration study predicted the policy would plunge millions of children into poverty. "If that brief authority is more important than the enduring principles of protecting children and childhood," he asked, "then what is to be said of those who prefer the one to the other?" The question was whether the nation would maintain "the national commitment to dependent children": "If this administration wishes to go down in history as one that abandoned, eagerly abandoned [that commitment], so be it. I would not want to be associated with such an enterprise, and I shall not be."[5]

Moynihan's writings recast the problem of poverty creatively. "The issue of welfare is the issue of dependency," he declared in *The Politics of a Guaranteed Income* (1973). "It is different from poverty." There were admirable qualities associated with being poor, he said, but none with being dependent.[6] It was with respect to poverty that he most liked to invoke the Catholic essayist Georges Bernanos's dictum that "the worst, the most corrupting lies are problems poorly stated."[7] A critic of the micromanagerial approach that characterized much of the War on Poverty—which sought to transform the lives of the poor rather than merely to alleviate their material distress—he would have preferred a simple strategy of income transfer. He began as a believer in the power of work to combat dependency but came to question whether, given the extent of social pathology in impoverished communities, full employment was still a cure. He asked in 1985: "What if employment had lost its power to determine social arrangements? What if deprivation, discrimination, had gone on too long? What if disorganization now sustained itself?"[8] Nonetheless, he continued to emphasize employment, as in the welfare reform bill he proposed in 1988.

In many ways, Moynihan's work on poverty assumes a quasi-tragic or at least a frustrating dimension, for several of his aspirations came tantalizingly near to realization only to be undone by politics or circumstance. The guaranteed income was almost achieved, yet politics—and then research suggesting it increased family breakup—undid it. His career-long devotion to welfare reform culminated in his opposition to a reform bill in 1995 and 1996 that he viewed as too radical and risky. But Moynihan's accomplishments in the area were also substantial. *One Third of a Nation,* the report he helped write in 1963 regarding massive failure rates on the mental test for draft-eligible men, called attention to the link between poverty and IQ and helped to galvanize the War on Poverty and guide other research. It has been said that the political storm that greeted his *Negro Family: The Case for National Action* (1965) froze scholarship on poverty and the African American family structure for a generation through sheer intimidation, but a subsequent thaw has vindicated his prescience.[9] It was Moynihan's Family Security Act of 1988, not the welfare reform of 1996, that unleashed the experiments in welfare reform at the state level that have been given so much credit for addressing the problem of dependency—experiments Moynihan felt could proceed without revoking the federal guarantee of benefits for dependent children.

Several themes unite Moynihan's ideas and work on poverty. First, as mentioned earlier, Moynihan believed in a national commitment to antipoverty measures as a matter of both policy and morality. His moral commitment manifested in his passion about the issue of poverty—a passion that lasted throughout his career, even in an age when most politics was obsessed with the middle class, and strikingly overwhelmed Moynihan's concern about other groups; he was, for example, relentlessly unsympathetic to the middle-class service providers whom he saw as siphoning money from the poor. When he was accosted by a group of Harvard students over the Nixon administration's cuts to social spending in areas such as education, he responded that the students, future teachers doubtless among them, were "defending a class interest."[10] Moynihan's policy commitment arose from a fear that state-by-state differentials in benefits would trigger a "race to the bottom" in which states would underbid one another's welfare benefits to avoid attracting beneficiaries.

Second, Moynihan persistently denied a causal link between poverty programs and social pathologies. He emphasized that he had established the deterioration of the African American family based on data collected before Johnson's poverty program was even conceived. Moreover, he rejected as unproven the claim that welfare caused nonmarital births, noting that rates of those births were climbing "in all the industrial nations of the North Atlantic," regardless of their welfare policies,[11] and that they continued to climb in the United States even as the real value of welfare benefits plunged in the 1970s and 1980s. This was the central conservative truth—that culture rather than politics determined the success of a society—in action. Moynihan was a particular critic of Charles Murray's *Losing Ground,* which on its publication in 1984 became a seminal source for those who claimed a causal connection between poverty programs and social problems.[12] "Murray raises some interesting questions," Moynihan asserted the next year. "He makes various assertions consistent with what is already known, but *he fails to prove anything.*"[13] *Losing Ground,* he argued, "attributes developments . . . to government actions that mostly began after these developments had commenced as clearly recognizable statistical trends."[14] That was not to say Moynihan was closed to the possibility that poverty programs had accelerated or otherwise contributed to dependency. "We owe it to one another," he said, "to be honest and open on this point."[15] But the connection had not been *proved,* and he believed we equally owed it to ourselves to rely on facts rather than supposition, especially if the supposition was politically informed.

Indeed, though Moynihan has often been associated with the idea that Great Society programs had not achieved their aim, his consistent complaint was that they—and later welfare efforts—did not spend enough on the poor, not that they indulged too much. To the extent the government had spent money on the poor, such as through Social Security, it had achieved immense successes in mitigating poverty. Moynihan consistently argued that the transition from dependency to work would require an investment of additional resources. Moreover, he was an advocate of poor families and especially children whose falling and "grossly inadequate" benefits pinned them below the poverty line.

Third, Moynihan argued that the family rather than the individual should be the unit of analysis in the study of poverty and of economic well-being more generally. This view was closely connected to his debts to Catholic social thought, which emphasized the primacy of family as an acculturating and, importantly, buffering institution standing between the individual and the state. The alternative was a raw individualism that projected a false image of the person excerpted from social and especially familial circumstance. This perspective enabled Moynihan's insight that "poverty [was] inextricably associated with family structure" (which was not to say the broken family was its sole medium),[16] as well as an array of proposed solutions that were intended, in a variety of ways, to strengthen families as a means of combating dependency. This was an expression of his commitment to subsidiarity: empowering families to solve social problems within their competence would strengthen them, whereas bypassing families would weaken them. The family was one of many subsidiary institutions, he observed—one "that mediates between the individual and the state, that suggests an antidote to alienation, an end to anomie, and a curb on secular statism."[17] He was acutely aware of the centrality of cultural influences such as family breakdown in poverty, crime, and other sociological phenomena, and for that reason, he was profoundly concerned about the erosion of cultural standards that seemed to normalize behavior once recognized as deviant. The family was the vehicle for the transmission not merely of material wealth—though that was vital—but also of cultural norms. As he learned from his careful analysis of James Coleman's lengthy study on educational equality during the faculty seminar he led on the topic at Harvard, family stability was the single most important factor, more important even than schools, in determining educational success as well.

The "tangle of pathology" that arose from the collapse of family structure was a condition, in turn, of "post-industrialism," a state in which the flight to cities of poor populations amid the simultaneous disappearance of urban jobs led to dislocation and alienation. The suddenness of this flight, he and Glazer had written as early as 1963, was "immensely disruptive of traditional social patterns," as evidenced by the Irish slums of the nineteenth century.[18] Amid postindustrial conditions, manufacturing jobs were disappearing, which was battering families, especially children—a phenomenon that often took the form of welfare dependency. This postindustrial pattern of vulnerable children and fragile families seemed untethered from macroeconomic conditions, so that "marital instability and tenuous labor markets [would] leave a fair number of children poor even in prosperous countries."[19]

At its core and from the perspective of policy, Moynihan also understood poverty in terms of material privation, a seemingly self-evident proposition but for the extent to which the War on Poverty came to distort it. He did not define poverty in terms of a lack of services or of power, although he recognized its association with these factors. He thus argued consistently for "get[ting] more money directly into the hands of the poor." Later, having credited Democrats with their decades-long advocacy for the poor, he also praised "the clarity with which some Republicans at least perceive[d] poverty as a condition of not having enough money."[20]

Moynihan appears to have believed, at least in the 1960s and 1970s, in something like a causal relationship between poverty and social disorganization, such that relieving the former would also alleviate the latter. Discussing the Coleman Report, he therefore noted that "the most promising alternative [for improving educational outcomes] would be to alter the way in which parents deal with their children at home. Unfortunately, it is not obvious how this could be done." Without further explanation, he went on to say that "income maintenance, family allowances, etc., seem a logical beginning."[21] How precisely this linkage might operate was unclear. The suggestion is not that Moynihan viewed income as a panacea. On the contrary, he listed it as only one part of a multivariate approach to ending dependency that included full employment, social services, curtailment of racial discrimination, and other factors.[22] But he does seem to have imputed some causal power to it either to alter behavior or to create conditions in which behavior would change.

Detecting the unstated premises beneath this claim requires speculation that can, at best, be merely informed. James Patterson has identified the bottom line in Moynihan's argument—"without decent income for the male breadwinner, many families would fall apart"—yet the underlying assumption remains elusive.[23] The closest Moynihan came to an explanation was a reference in *The Politics of a Guaranteed Income* to his "hope" that "the provision of income support for 'intact' families would in some way lessen the strains of life at the margin," thus implying both that he guessed the strain was the problem and that he recognized he was guessing.[24] But amid an enormous set of questions that were and remain unanswered, this is a thesis he seems ultimately to have abandoned, perhaps in response to data suggesting the guaranteed income encouraged family dissolution. In any case, by 1986, though he argued that a guaranteed income could have alleviated poverty, he also observed that it would not have eliminated social disorganization.[25]

Finally, Moynihan insisted that poverty policy be rooted in evidence. Significantly, as his career progressed and as evidence accumulated, his appreciation for social science's complexity—and the daunting complexity of the social systems it sought to analyze—mounted. He became dismissive of sweeping, single-shot reforms from both the Right and the Left, especially to the extent they claimed to be based on social science. In the Reagan era—whose mood was captured by the president's quip that "in the war on poverty, poverty won"[26]—Moynihan dismissed the thesis that antipoverty programs exacerbated poverty as arrogant and anticonservative pseudoscience that reduced complex social systems to simple theorems: "We are seeing at work in both 'liberal' Democratic and 'conservative' Republican administrations the demon that Michael Oakeshott has identified as Rationalism—the great heresy of modern times."[27] His use of quotation marks around the words *liberal* and *conservative* suggests his belief that adherents were being true to neither tradition. Later, dismissing the 1995–1996 welfare reform as similarly pseudoscientific and utopian, he implored: "Scholars have been working at these issues for years now, and the more capable they are, the more tentative and incremental their findings."[28]

The story of Moynihan's commitment to the dependent poor and the ideas he generated in the process unfolds in three acts: the idealism of the War on Poverty and the controversy of the Moynihan Report; the guaranteed income; and, finally, the welfare reform he pursued throughout and ultimately opposed at the end of his Senate career.

THE WAR ON POVERTY AND THE MOYNIHAN REPORT

Moynihan's first foray into poverty policy at the national level came with the January 1964 report *One Third of a Nation,* the product of President Kennedy's Task Force on Manpower Conservation, which Moynihan served as secretary. "[The report] was in many ways," he later reflected, "the first profile of poverty the federal government had yet developed. The linkage between failure on the mental tests [for induction into the armed forces] with the common indices of poverty was striking."[29] The alarming data helped galvanize LBJ's War on Poverty, which commenced with his State of the Union address that month.

Moynihan was part of Labor Secretary Willard Wirtz's working group, which compiled a proposal for President Johnson. Influenced by his own experience of childhood poverty, he believed, along with his Labor Department colleagues, in an "income strategy" as opposed to a "services strategy"—that is, one that would transfer resources directly to the poor. Within weeks, he saw that the whole effort was doomed. He reflected in 1986:

> Mind, I had no illusion that anything much would come of LBJ's War on Poverty. . . . I had attended the cabinet meeting of March 16, 1964 at which our proposals were presented. Our centerpiece was to be a big jobs program, financed by an increase in tobacco taxes. The President heard us this far, pronounced that the administration was cutting taxes not raising them, and reaching for the telephone attached to the underside of the cabinet table, turned sideways and got through to some hapless committee chairman or whomever, leaving the cabinet to understand that the discussion of poverty had concluded.[30]

Worse than this lack of commitment, though, was the tack the battle took: guerrilla warfare rather than a frontal assault. The War on Poverty became obsessed with—in Theodore J. Lowi's formulation—eliminating rather than alleviating poverty, a goal that required not merely providing money to the poor but also attempting to transform and micromanage their lives.[31] Consequently, the services strategy—impelled by heady and flawed social science—prevailed. The jobs program was passed over in favor of community action, a concept based on stimulating political involvement among the poor by involving them in decisions about how poverty program funds were spent. The idea, in the words of the law, was that the poverty program should be implemented with the "maximum feasible participation" of the communities it affected. Moynihan later derided the program as being based less on genuine social science than on "the imputation of guilt on the part of the larger society."[32]

His lacerating, book-length critique of the concept, *Maximum Feasible Misunderstanding* (1969), characterized the government as flailing about, partnering with such organizations as the New York City–based Mobilization for Youth, which "reeked of the notion of the proletariat."[33] Community action, which stoked the unrest simmering in the cities in the name of organizing the poor, became an ideology whose mostly middle-class adherents "acquired an *interest* in the political turmoil of the moment and came very near to misusing [their] position to advance that interest."[34] However, political organizing was not the proper role of public employees, Moynihan observed: "Social radicalism is not a civil service calling."[35]

His early commitment to subsidiarity was evident in his stated preference in *Maximum Feasible Misunderstanding* for having the government, rather than directly organizing the poor, both encourage private trade union organizations that could operate independently once established, on one hand, and work with the churches already woven into the fabric of poor communities, on the other. "Or was it," he asked, "that hymn-shouting and bible-thumping somehow does not elicit in the fancies of the white radical quite the same fascination as does the black demi-monde?"[36] During this period, he argued in the book, "the great failing of the Johnson administration was that an immense opportunity to institute more or less permanent social changes—a fixed full employment program, a measure of income maintenance—was lost while energies were expended in ways that probably hastened the end of the brief period when such options were open."[37]

In an essay published in 1972, Moynihan cited statistics indicating that if one-third of the money spent on poverty programs had been "given directly to the poor, there would no longer be any poverty in the United States."[38] Instead, however, the money was going to social workers, teachers, and others who were primarily middle-class professionals. Moynihan noted the irony: for the first five years of the poverty program, a third of it was financed by taxes collected from the poor, and these funds were substantially used "to hire middle-class persons to be of assistance to poor persons." Consequently, "the actual *income transfer effect* of many of these . . . programs was to take money from farm laborers and give it to college graduates."[39] Similarly, he said, because teachers benefited from educational expenditures, increasing them would "*have the short-run effect of increasing income inequality.*"[40] The poverty programs were "more or less ingenious instances of that old technique: feed the horses in order to nourish the sparrows that are in the vicinity. The horses have always found this plausible."[41] Professionals such as social workers and teachers performed admirable services, he was quick to add, and they were and should be well compensated. But noting that 71 percent of social workers said they chose their profession for "humanitarian" reasons, Moynihan warned against sanctimony: "Now one would wish this. It is surely a good thing for caseworkers to see themselves in this light. Or almost surely. But it tends to confuse public debate. Shoe-factory workers in Manchester, almost certainly earning considerably less than social workers in the same city, are not permitted to declare that they have chosen their profession for humanitarian reasons."[42]

The alternative to hiring professionals to minister to families was to invest directly in those families. The urgency of doing so, especially for

African Americans, arose from the fact that their families were eroding to the point of collapse—something Moynihan had discovered in what would become the most explosive and controversial episode of his career: the Moynihan Report.

Over the 1964–1965 winter, after he asked his staff at the Labor Department to explore the relationship between unemployment and the state of the African American family, Moynihan and his team made a startling discovery. The number of Aid to Families with Dependent Children cases among African Americans had become untethered from the unemployment rate; previously, the two metrics had risen and fallen in relative unison. But after 1963, AFDC cases among African Americans continued to rise even though unemployment fell. Moynihan's friend James Q. Wilson would dub this phenomenon "Moynihan's scissors." Given the relationship between AFDC cases and family breakup, Moynihan forecast a growing problem: family disintegration and what—in the Moynihan Report of 1965, *The Negro Family: The Case for National Action*—he would warn of as "a new crisis in race relations."[43] Despite the fact that Moynihan laid the blame squarely on the legacy of slavery as well as ongoing discrimination, he was dogged through the rest of his life by charges of having "blamed the victim" instead.

After establishing the basic contours of the problem and describing recent African American advances in civil rights, the Moynihan Report turned to a searching reflection on the tension between liberty and equality. "The fundamental problem here," Moynihan wrote, "is that the Negro revolution . . . is a movement for equality as well as for liberty":

> Liberty and Equality are the twin ideals of American democracy, but they are not the same thing. Nor, most importantly, are they equally attractive to all groups at any given time; nor yet are they always compatible one with the other.
>
> Many persons who would gladly die for liberty are appalled by equality. Many who are devoted to equality are puzzled and even troubled by liberty. Much of the political history of the American nation can be seen as a competition between these two ideals.[44]

In the report, Moynihan acknowledged the difference between equality of opportunity and equality of results. Whites had tended to see the former as a manifestation of liberty, he wrote, but African Americans were now demanding equality in fact or, in other words, equality of results. Consequently, "the principal challenge of the next phase of the Negro revolution is to make certain that equality of results will now follow. If we do not, there will be no social peace in the United States for generations."[45]

A key to that equality would be the restoration of the "crumbling" African American family. Through this lens, we can view some of Moynihan's earliest insights into the primacy of family as the building block of society. As he put it, "The family is the basic social unit of American life; it is the basic socializing unit. By and large, adult conduct in society is learned as a child."[46] Contrary to later accusations, Moynihan did not overgeneralize about "the" African American family. Instead, he observed that African Americans were "dividing between a stable middle-class group that is steadily growing stronger and more successful, and an increasingly disorganized and disadvantaged lower-class group."[47] Nonmarital births among African Americans had risen from 16.8 to 23.6 percent between 1940 and 1963; in the same period, such births grew from 2 to 3.07 percent for whites. A quarter of African American families were headed by women, and only a minority of African American children were reaching the age of eighteen having lived all their lives with both parents. In turn, this family pattern led to a "startling increase in welfare dependency," which further fueled family breakdown. Fathers were absent in two-thirds of AFDC families.[48]

Moynihan attributed the problem to the lingering effects of the particularly harsh and dehumanizing American strain of chattel slavery, which destroyed the African American family and "broke the will of the Negro people."[49] Then, with emancipation, "the Negro was given liberty, but not equality. Life remained hazardous and marginal. Of the greatest importance, the Negro male, particularly in the South, became an object of intense hostility." Moreover, Moynihan asserted, "segregation, and the submissiveness it exacts, is surely more destructive to the male than to the female personality," thereby undermining the emergence of strong fathers: "The very essence of the male animal, from the bantam rooster to the four-star general, is to strut."[50] Moynihan's situation of the problem within a social and historical context has not dissuaded critics from accusing him of blaming individuals, to the point of being racist and sexist.[51] But he himself would later reflect that he had gone so far out of his way to avert this that he might, on the contrary, have instead been accused of "almost misstating evidence in order to avoid any implication of blame."[52]

The fact that the African American community had survived centuries of abuse was a tribute to its strength, Moynihan's report continued, but it had "paid a fearful price" in the form of "a tangle of pathology" that "entrapped" youth and from which few escaped for more than a generation. "In essence," he stated, "the Negro community has been forced into a matriarchal structure which, because it is so out of line with the rest of American society, seriously retards the progress of the group as a whole, and imposes a crushing burden on the Negro male and, in consequence, on a great many Negro women as well."[53] The essence of the problem lay not with female-headed households per se but rather with the mismatch between the authority structure African American children encountered in the home and the one they encountered in the larger society. And, Moynihan added, "ours is a society which presumes male leadership in private and public affairs."[54]

This obviously no longer being the case, it would be interesting to know how Moynihan would write the passage today. At some level, the problem with single parenthood was less related to gender than to what would later be described as "task overload,"[55] but he clearly believed male authority to be inherently important. As late as 1995 in an interview with Peggy Noonan on PBS, he would say: "We have lost a family structure capable of disciplining young males. It is the most difficult thing in any society. It's universally difficult. There is a nice African saying that it takes a whole village to raise a child. But it does at least take one male present."[56]

The Moynihan Report made clear that there was "absolutely no question of any genetic differential" in intelligence. It argued, instead, that "American society . . . impairs Negro potential,"[57] as evidenced by statistics on delinquency and crime among African American men; their higher failure rate on the mental test for the armed forces; and the general phenomenon of alienation among African American men as measured by withdrawal from social institutions such as the workforce, schools, and churches.

Concluding with a call for "national action," Moynihan specified that the intent of the report had "been to define a problem, rather than propose solutions to it."[58] Yet after the report was leaked, he was accused of diagnosing pathologies but offering no treatments. Still, the report's analysis did propose that a "general strategy" was necessary to address a problem defined as follows: "Three centuries of injustice have brought about deep-seated structural distortions in the life of the Negro American. At this point, the present tangle of pathology is capable of perpetuating itself without assistance from the white world. The cycle can be broken only if these distortions are set right."[59]

These distortions, the report made clear, stemmed from the problem of family structure, and this was the proper object of a national policy. In one of the earliest instances of his preference for policy over program, Moynihan therefore suggested that the government adopt a national policy of bringing African Americans to "full and equal sharing" in citizenship. "To this end," he stated, "the programs of the federal government bearing on this objective shall be designed to have the effect, directly or indirectly, of enhancing the stability and resources of the Negro American family."[60]

Distributed within the government in the spring of 1965, the report led to an address by President Johnson at Howard University that June. Moynihan cowrote it. Johnson would look back on the speech as his finest civil rights address. It read, in part:

Equal opportunity is essential, but not enough, not enough. Men and women of all races are born with the same range of abilities. But ability is not just the product of birth. Ability is stretched or stunted by the family that you live with, and the neighborhood you live in—by the school you go to and the poverty or the richness of your surroundings. It is the product of a hundred unseen forces playing upon the little infant, the child, and finally the man.[61]

The president promised to call a White House conference on the topic, but before it convened, the report itself—which was written as an internal government document to guide the Johnson administration's policy making—was leaked, and a political firestorm ensued. The conference was largely abortive. Moynihan, meanwhile, left the administration to run unsuccessfully for president of the New York City Council, but he continued to push for a focus on family policy. He published a long essay on the topic that fall in the liberal Catholic journal *America*. There, he noted that modern economics seemed to be capable of producing sustained prosperity but that a substantial part of the population had been left out of it; at the same time, he argued, prosperity itself might also be "producing much of our poverty." He suggested that both problems might "in fact [be] part of a single phenomenon: the pathology of post-industrial society." This was the new challenge for social policy.

Picking up on the Catholic theme of the family as the basic unit of social organization, he noted that social policy had up to that point been directed at the individual. Unemployment statistics, the minimum wage, and other facets of the federal government were agnostic, for example, as to the number of children in a family, treating a parent with, say, seven children and another with three as comparably situated. "This is a pattern that is almost uniquely American," he observed. "Most of the industrial democracies of the world have adopted a wide range of social programs designed specifically to support the stability and viability of the family."[62] The consequences of ignoring this need, he wrote in *America*, were bleak:

From the wild Irish slums of the 19th-century Eastern seaboard, to the riot-torn suburbs of Los Angeles, there is one unmistakable lesson in American history: a community that allows a large number of young men to grow up in broken families, dominated by women, never acquiring any stable relationship to male authority, never acquiring any set of rational expectations about the future—that community asks for and gets chaos. Crime, violence, unrest, disorder—most particularly the furious, unrestrained lashing out at the whole social structure—that is not only to be expected; it is very near to inevitable. And it is richly deserved.[63]

A national family policy would recognize, as Moynihan wrote two years later and repeatedly affirmed, Alva Myrdal's observation that government always had policies affecting families, whether they were explicit or latent; the question was merely whether they were rational. "*A nation without a conscious family policy leaves to chance and mischance an area of social reality of the utmost importance, which in consequence will be exposed to the untrammeled and frequently thoroughly undesirable impact of other forces,*" he wrote in a foreword to a new edition of Myrdal's *Nation and Family* in 1967.[64] Families were paramount. As President Johnson had noted in the speech Moynihan cowrote, "The family is the cornerstone of our society. More than any other force it shapes the attitude, the hopes, the ambitions, and the values of the child. And when the family collapses it is the children that are usually damaged. When it happens on a massive scale the community itself is crippled."[65]

Family policy thus had to address itself, Moynihan wrote, not merely to "the rudiments of physical well-being . . . but also [to] providing the conditions of early life which produce emotionally stable personalities."[66] The content of family policy remained elusive for him; it was the mere fact of having a policy that he felt would galvanize action. For instance, having such a policy would require the president or his designee to report to Congress regularly on the state of the American family. "I had precious little idea as to what a family policy would amount to," he reflected in 1985, "but had in mind the example of the Employment Act of 1946. All that this legislation actually did was to create the Council of

Economic Advisors. Yet it had had far greater impact than any 'jobs bill.'"[67] A family policy would recognize "a primary social reality" whose "intellectual" denial he denounced, "namely that family structure and functioning have consequences for children, and that, by and large, families function best in traditional arrangements."[68]

The problem, Moynihan wrote disapprovingly, was that liberalism had absorbed from its laissez-faire ancestry a belief that individuals should be unshackled from any oppressive institution, the family included. The issue for Moynihan was Tocquevillian; the family was a buffer between the individual and the state. Tocqueville had warned of the tendency of democratic society to devolve into the twin poles of state and individual, with the latter dependent solely on the former and degraded, subservient, and enervated as a result. Hence, for him as for Moynihan, mediating institutions were paramount. Moynihan now seemed to see something like Tocqueville's bleak vision coming true. In *The Politics of a Guaranteed Income* (1973), he wrote of "a general development in social thought, liberal on the one hand, Marxist on the other, which increasingly concentrated attention either on the lone individual or on abstract collectivities—the market, the electorate, the state, the universe—all to the exclusion of the family in between."[69] Yet the ascendant ethos of individualism, Moynihan worried, overlooked the centrality of family. Worse, it implicitly blamed any failure on the individual him- or herself. Meanwhile, at the opposite pole, humanists fearful of stigmatizing the poor were reluctant to acknowledge problems with their families.[70]

In the *America* article, Moynihan began to hint at a solution to the dilemma of family dissolution—and at a festering dissatisfaction with the programmatic approach of the War on Poverty:

Project Headstart, a program in the war on poverty, is one of the most imaginative and promising efforts to bring hope to slum children that we have seen in this generation. Even so, it must be stated that we are paying women—well-qualified, professional women to be sure—up to $9.20 an hour to look after the children of men who can't make $1.50. If the working-class fathers of the city earned a steady $3.00 or $4.00 an hour, would we need a Project Headstart?[71]

Moynihan's solution, in other words, was to direct jobs and resources directly to the poor.

In *The Negro Family*, Moynihan had discussed evidence suggesting that financial stability and family stability were linked: "Higher incomes are unmistakably associated with greater family stability—which comes first may be a matter for conjecture, but the conjunction of the two characteristics is unmistakable."[72] Elsewhere, he emphasized that "the essential fact about family stability (contrary to a good deal of folklore) is that as individuals become more prosperous, in the sense of having greater incomes, their marriages become more stable."[73] Conversely, in a *Public Interest* article in 1989, he invoked Ralf Dahrendorf's argument that inequality arises from the disparate success of groups and individuals in complying with social norms, noting that even though American society rewarded traditional families, it "punishe[d] those that in the past would have been called deviant. . . . The disjunction between our norms and our behavior is dysfunctional in the extreme."[74] Family structure, he speculated, "may now prove to be the principal conduit of social class status. Family structure will prove, I suspect, to be the primary setting in which social capital, as James S. Coleman uses the term, is amassed or dissipated. Social capital makes for education, access, mobility, ensuring that talent is rewarded."[75]

But this understanding was lost, he complained, on advocates of community action. The government was spending billions on poverty programs, money that was ultimately going into the pockets of middle-class service providers, when, in fact, higher incomes might in and of themselves help stabilize families. He again argued that what was needed was to "get more money directly into the hands of the poor." And for that journey, the fastest forward-moving train departed from Richard Nixon's White House.

THE GUARANTEED INCOME

After his unsuccessful run for the presidency of the New York City Council in 1965, Moynihan returned to academia. Then, in 1969, he shocked even close friends by joining the Nixon White House as counselor to the president for urban affairs. But Moynihan did not, as has been supposed,[76] defect to the Nixon administration out of disgust with the Democratic excesses of the 1960s. That narrative is hospitable to the neoconservative portrayal of Moynihan, but it simply does not square with his own understanding of his motives. He believed that Nixon provided an intriguing path forward for his ideas, whereas Democrats had ideologically exhausted themselves. He would later reflect that the Johnson administration opposed a guaranteed income "not because it was politically risky, but primarily because the men in charge did not believe in such boldness. The Democrats had become the party of timidity."[77] But that did not mean Moynihan had in any sense grown conservative; if anything, his worry was that Democrats had. As James Q. Wilson observed, "He served in two Democratic and two Republican administrations, not because he had no views but because he persuaded the presidents in each case that their views should move toward his."[78] Of his relationship with Nixon, Moynihan wrote that the idea with respect to poverty policy was to "move beyond a *services* strategy to an approach that provides inducements to move from a dependent and deficient status to one of independence and sufficiency. Essentially, this is an *income* strategy, based fundamentally on the provision of incentives to increase the earnings and to expand the property base of the poorest groups."[79]

The difference between an income strategy and a services strategy most vividly illustrates the distinction between New Deal and Great Society liberalism, and this distinction is vital to an accurate perception of Moynihan's thought. It is important to note, however, that he did not approach the War on Poverty from a posture of apology. This, among other points, would distinguish him from other Democrats in the 1990s. He recognized that for all its shortcomings, the effort proceeded from noble motives and fed hungry children. But it was different. It provided services designed to transform the lives of impoverished people. The essence of the New Deal, by contrast, was an income strategy: the elderly, for example, were poor, so society gave them money, and by the 1980s, poverty among the elderly had been drastically reduced.

The core of the income strategy Moynihan envisioned would be an allowance based on family size, administered in the form of a negative income tax. The idea illustrates the unique ground he occupied ideologically: devoted to subsidiarity—in this case, to the family—but also to the idea that the public sector could play a constructive role in nourishing subsidiary institutions if it acknowledged their importance. Moynihan had already expressed his desire for a coordinated family policy and, crucially, he observed that the nation *had* a tacit one in Aid to Families with Dependent Children. That New Deal era welfare program provided a federal entitlement of support to single-parent families, building on state programs in a formula that changed over time based on state law. But, he stressed, it was a family allowance for "*broken* families. Each family is given a sum of money according to its needs, as measured by its size. But only *after* the family breaks up."[80] He believed an income policy might have a wide array of effects, such as long-term improvements in education through "improved nutrition, clothing and living conditions."[81] There were, as has been seen, intriguing indications that higher income might correlate with family stability, which the comprehensive Coleman study had shown to be the only real variable reliably associated with educational achievement.

Moynihan, who had supported such policies as early as 1964, noted that all other industrial democracies had family allowances that recognized the wage system's indifference to family size.[82] Family allowances, in turn, were "a system for redistributing income in such a way as to benefit the child-rearing portion of a nation's population." Unlike the services approach, he said, a family allowance required no serious bureaucracy to administer since it would be paid automatically. It would thus "involve the Federal government's doing what it did best, namely, the collection of taxes and redistribution of income. Seek simplicity, Whitehead . . . had ordained. Thereafter distrust it, but first seek it."[83]

In announcing the Family Assistance Plan (FAP), President Nixon explained the program in terms of the following steps. A family of four with no income would receive $1,600. It could keep $60 a month of earnings without losing FAP benefits, after which the benefits would be reduced by $0.50 on the dollar. The head of a working family would also receive benefits—a family of five earning $2,000 a year, for instance, would receive $1,260. The benefit would phase out beyond an income of $3,920 for a family of four—just above the federal poverty rate.[84]

FAP was, in a sense, the completion of the New Deal's social insurance agenda, extending the principle of Social Security to families with children. Moreover, "it [was] provided not for adults, but for children, in response to the one fact that any group can be brought to agree on, namely that kids cost money."[85] Crucially, Moynihan pointed out, "the striking feature of the [guaranteed income] idea is that it introduced incentives for the poor to increase their incomes" because, unlike welfare, the allowance was reduced but, for the working poor, not completely eliminated in response to extra earnings. By contrast, due to the costs of child care and other expenses of employment, welfare recipients under the existing apparatus faced a disincentive to work unless their potential earnings would far outstrip their benefits.[86]

Moynihan wrote in a memo to the president:

> *The essential fact about the [Family Assistance Plan] is that it will abolish poverty for dependent children and the working poor.* The cost is not very great. *Because it is a direct payment system.* The tremendous costs of the poverty program come from *services....*
>
> The [Family Assistance Plan] would enable you to begin cutting back sharply on these costly and questionable services, and yet to assert with full validity that it was under your Presidency that poverty was abolished in America.[87]

The narrative Moynihan wove in *The Politics of a Guaranteed Income,* which he wrote after leaving the Nixon White House, described a program that came near to passage, only to be squeezed to its demise between conservatives who found it too generous and liberals who complained it was insufficiently so. It was also the closest Moynihan ever came to the pursuit of a simple solution to a complex social problem. In that respect, it appears un-Burkean. In the years leading up to the guaranteed income, Moynihan himself had seemingly warned of such an outcome, and he had done so in Burkean terms, predicting that "the cost of transforming the [welfare] system would disrupt a vast array of entrenched social arrangements."[88] He suggested in this period that there was instead an opportunity to "make a number of important, incremental advances." "Radical change," by contrast, was "a danger."[89]

But the guaranteed income certainly seems transformative, if not outright radical. Indeed, Moynihan would write of it in what appeared to be explicitly anti-Burkean terms: "The inability of policy-makers to comprehend the complex effects of large changes can be seen as an argument for making only small ones, but the FAP experience of little knowledge impelling a fundamental reform should be seen as an important modification of a general rule." Still, the essence of prudence lies in the calibration of action to circumstance. Burke was capable of daring when circumstance demanded it, and it is significant that Moynihan invoked his old teacher Oakeshott in this context: "'Politics,' Michael Oakeshott has written, 'is not the science of setting up a permanently impregnable society.' It is at most a matter of prevailing over dangers near enough to be perceived, which may, at times, dictate ambitious enterprise, such as Family Assistance. Qualities of energy and courage are at least as relevant for success as power of analysis."[90]

In a sense, moreover, the dimension of the problem to which Moynihan addressed himself *was* simple and thus apparently susceptible to a daring solution. To the extent the essence of poverty was material privation, material relief seemed the logical remedy. He would thus later reflect that had the guaranteed income legislation been enacted, "it is arguably the case that there would be no significant poverty in the United States. Social disorganization, yes. But not poverty defined as a level of income."[91] Still, social disorganization was part of the point. As he suggested as early as 1965 in *The Negro Family*, Moynihan hoped that an income strategy would help to stabilize families and mitigate the social pathologies that, at that point in his career, he took to be the product of poverty.[92] He also understood the core pathology to be not poverty but dependency, a problem he thought the guaranteed income program would help overcome because of its comparatively strong work incentives.

Interestingly, Moynihan's own perception of the Family Assistance Plan in this respect seemed nearly split. On the one hand, he acknowledged its radicalism, describing it as "'fundamental,' rather than merely 'incremental,' social change."[93] Yet, on the other hand, he also insisted that "it was not accompanied by any especially large promises" as to its effects, and his description of the public disposition toward it sounded quasi Burkean. "In effect," he wrote, "the public asked little more than that change be accompanied by continuity and deference to traditional proprieties: no great condition to impose in a period of continuous and rapid transformation, especially in technological matters."[94] He apparently believed the guaranteed income would meet these criteria, though Moynihan himself told Nixon it would abolish poverty, certainly a large promise, and many critics of FAP thought of it as a giveaway in tension with traditional proprieties.

It must be said, moreover, that as soon as evidence emerged that contradicted his hopes for the guaranteed income, Moynihan abandoned it. Government social scientists had conducted a multiyear controlled assessment of the effects of income maintenance (the Seattle/Denver Income Maintenance Experiment, or SIME-DIME), and when they reported that results showed these transfers actually increased family breakup, Moynihan, then a freshman senator, exclaimed frankly: "Were we wrong about guaranteed income! Seemingly it is calamitous. It increases family dissolution by 70 percent, decreases work, etc. Such is now the state of science, and it seems to me we are honor-bound to abide by it at the moment."[95]

What was now left to Moynihan was the task that occupied much of his Senate career from 1977 to 2001—reforming the existing welfare system while battling, sometimes desperately, to preserve a national commitment to the dependent poor.

SENATE REFORMER

"Is this nation, entering its third century," Moynihan asked the Special House Subcommittee on Welfare Reform in 1977, "now ready to try to ensure that its children as a matter of national policy will have a decent home life?" The terms of the question frame Moynihan's attitude toward welfare reform for the whole of his Senate career, emphasizing the primacy of children, the centrality of the family ("a decent home life"), and the necessity of a *national* policy. The problem, as he saw it, was that Aid to Families with Dependent Children "has failed. It breaks up families, discourages work, and provides, in some places, grossly inadequate levels of living." The criteria of success that would guide Moynihan's attempts at and then ultimate resistance to reform are evident here: welfare needed to encourage family stability and work *and*, crucially, provide an adequate living—which, given the state-by-state patchwork that encouraged policy makers to bid down benefits to avoid attracting beneficiaries, it often failed to do.[96]

As early as 1978, Moynihan was pushing to permit state-level experimentation with welfare policies while assuming national responsibility for benefits. "Welfare is a national responsibility, and the national government should bear the primary burden of paying for it," he argued as he introduced his State and Local Welfare Reform and Fiscal Relief Act that year. He added that states should be given the freedom to design innovative welfare programs. The bill was also "in the liberal tradition. It would allow significant improvements in welfare benefits," especially in areas where they were inadequate.[97] Critics ranging from the *New York Times* to the *Nation*—Richard A. Cloward and Frances Fox Piven, writing in the latter in 1979, viciously attacked Moynihan and claimed his colleagues treated him as "a clown"—complained that his bill did not sufficiently guarantee that extra funds would be used on extra benefits.[98]

In the 1980s, much of Moynihan's energy on this issue was expended in opposing the Reagan administration's proposals to curtail the national role in welfare. The necessity of a national role was *the* lesson, he argued, of the history of welfare, and the administration's proposal to "swap" responsibility for welfare in exchange for a federal takeover of Medicaid was "nonsense as federalism and bankrupt as policy. By getting 'welfare' out of Washington, the Administration hopes to obscure a problem, not to deal with one," he charged.[99] He felt the administration had learned the wrong lesson from the 1960s, which was not that poverty had triumphed in the war on it but rather that the problem required subtler solutions that appreciated the complexity of social systems. Again he argued: "We need a rebirth of social policy as both a moral and an empirical exercise, free of the mindless millennialism of the past and the equally thoughtless meanness of the present, and conscious also of what can be the cost of merely good intentions."[100]

The meanness to which Moynihan referred—he once accused the Reagan administration of "terminal sleaze" for attempting to reduce benefits for people who received charitable donations—arose in part from what he regarded as the disprovable thesis that the Great Society not only failed to solve poverty but also actually exacerbated it. Reagan said in a radio broadcast in 1983: "There is no question that many well-intentioned Great Society–type programs contributed to family breakups, welfare dependency, and a large increase in births out of wedlock."[101] The problem from Moynihan's perspective, as we have seen, is that he forecast these trends in the Moynihan Report based on data compiled *before* the War on Poverty was launched, and they continued to intensify even as the value of welfare benefits precipitously fell during the 1970s and 1980s. Moreover, family dissolution was occurring across the Atlantic world, regardless of nations' welfare policies. The basic, commonsensical conditions of a causal link simply did not obtain.[102]

In the absence of conclusive data, the key for Moynihan was controlled experimentation and careful analysis, always while attending to the needs of the poor—especially poor children. Proceeding in this fog required prudence. The statesman could not avoid the inherent difficulty of choices. Moynihan contended:

What is not needed, in any event, is a response to the dilemma of welfare dependency that repeals the social insurance programs of the New Deal. If we have learned anything from the story of Roosevelt's "one-third of a nation," it is that the perplexity is likely to persist. Just how and why this is so may now be beyond the analytic powers of social science, yet it cannot be kept beyond the realm of public policy.[103]

In January 1987, Moynihan suggested that reform be guided by three principles. First, "the primary responsibility for child support rests with the child's parents," including support from absent fathers. Second, able-bodied custodial parents also bore a responsibility to work, and society, in turn, bore a responsibility to provide both training and other support (such as child care) that work required. Third and finally, government should provide a "time-limited child-support supplement" to custodial parents; after the time limits expired, parents should be required to work in public jobs in exchange for receiving support.

These principles formed the basis of his Family Support Act of 1988, which he described as a new social contract that would permit state-level experimentation while imposing work requirements on recipients. Significantly, two days before House-Senate conferees reached agreement on the bill, Moynihan was invoking social science to emphasize not the state of knowledge on the issue but rather the state of ignorance, which was what made experimentation necessary. "Roughly half our children, somewhat randomly, but inexorably, are born without a fair chance," he stated. "We know precious little about what to do about it. In a society with more than enough to go around, poverty is a form of bad luck. Children have the most of it."[104] By encouraging work, Moynihan said he hoped to reduce the stigma associated with welfare; by reducing the stigma, in turn, he hoped states would be encouraged to increase benefits, something the Reagan era deficits made impossible to do nationally, as he had long hoped.[105]

Ironically, it was the very success of the Family Support Act—"the Governors' Bill," as Moynihan called it—in stimulating a wave of experiments in the states that laid the groundwork for the Clinton era reform he would so passionately and sorrowfully oppose.

The stirrings of change emerged—inauspiciously, from Moynihan's perspective—in the get-tough language of the 1992 presidential campaign. President George H. W. Bush, facing a conservative challenge from Pat Buchanan in the Republican primaries, was promising to make welfare recipients work, something Moynihan said the Family Support Act already required. "Maybe he did not know," Moynihan offered charitably. "It is possible he did not know. I do not recall that he was at the Rose Garden signing ceremony, but he said he would do in legislation what we have already done."[106] Of President-elect Clinton's proposal to terminate AFDC benefits after two years, Moynihan remarked, "Put me down as anxious but willing." Success would require creating 1.5 million jobs.[107] But Clinton rejected Moynihan's advice to take up welfare reform at the beginning of his term, opting instead for his disastrous health care project, which culminated in the Republican takeover of Congress in the 1994 midterm elections. By the time welfare reform came to the fore in 1995 and 1996—with Clinton running for reelection—it was on terms Moynihan perceived as punitive and heartless. The national guarantee of aid to dependent children was to be abandoned.

The reform imposed a two-year consecutive limit on welfare benefits and a five-year lifetime cap, but critically, it also repealed the title of the Social Security Act guaranteeing a federal entitlement to welfare for impoverished children, replacing it with block grants to states. That supporters of the change defended it by pointing with satisfaction to the very state-level innovation that had only been possible because of his 1988 bill doubtless rankled Moynihan. The experimentation they sought was already happening under current law, yet they were congratulating themselves for enabling it. Moynihan's central objection was the abandonment of the underlying national commitment that his bill had retained—a matter to him, again, of both morality and policy—and he attempted desperately to alert his colleagues, especially Democrats, to the significance of the deed. "I had no idea how profoundly what used to be known as liberalism was shaken by the last election," he said. "No President, Republican or Democrat, in history, or 60 years' history, would dream of agreeing to the repeal of Title IV-A of Social Security. . . . Are there no serious persons in the Administration who can say, 'Stop, stop right now. No. We won't have this'?"[108]

Significantly, Moynihan characterized the reform as unconservative: "If conservative means anything, it means be careful, be thoughtful, and anticipate the unanticipated or understand that things will happen that you do not expect. And be very careful with the lives of children."[109] The reform reflected an exaggerated confidence in the state of knowledge as to welfare. He noted that one program, which was then in its fifth year and featured "very intensive counseling and training with respect to the issue of teen births," had been carefully evaluated and produced "no results. It is a very common encounter, when things as profound [as] human character and behavior are dealt with."[110] During one Senate debate, Moynihan held aloft a pen President Kennedy had given him from the 1963 signing (his last public one) of a bill that gradually emptied out mental hospitals in the name of reform and actually filled up the streets with mentally ill homeless people instead. "Give this a little thought, just a little thought," he implored, using the story as an illustration of unintended consequences flowing from well-intended reform.[111]

Democrats, for their part, had settled into a pattern of trading programmatic concessions with Republicans, "literally arranging flowers on the coffin of the provision for children in the Social Security Act. . . . Sixty years of program liberalism—a bill for you, a bill for me—had made this legislative behavior seem normal."[112] By the time the reform bill came to an initial vote, Moynihan was disgusted with the sheer emptiness of the moment. Looking from his desk in the Senate chamber, he could see clear to the Supreme Court on the opposite side of the Capitol complex, and he observed that not a single protester intervened—"not one of those flaunted, vaunted advocacy groups forever protecting the interests of the children and the helpless and the homeless and the what-you-will. . . . They should be ashamed. History will shame them."[113]

Moynihan has been accused of resorting to rhetorical excess in his condemnations of the bill. It was, he said, "bartering of the lives of babes"; he predicted children might end up "sleeping on grates"; and he remarked that "just how many infants we will put to the sword is not yet clear. There is dickering to do."[114] Moynihan's direst predictions clearly were not borne out, but several points must be raised against the general assumption that welfare reform succeeded despite Moynihan's gloomy pessimism. The first pertains to his accusation—laden with Burkean overtones—that risks with unforeseeable consequences were being taken with the well-being of children. The extent to which the risky strategy succeeded does not vindicate the morality of the gamble any more than an unethical medical experiment is exonerated by a fruitful outcome.

The second point is that, though a full assessment of the success or failure of welfare reform lies beyond the purview of this study, Moynihan did supply criteria by which the legislation could be tested. The narrative of welfare reform's success has generally relied on the number of people who have moved off welfare rolls and into the workforce—a valid metric, to be sure, and one that was impressive in the boom years of the late 1990s. But recall that for Moynihan, the crucial factors from his earliest days in the Senate—indeed, from his earliest acquaintance with the issue—were the extent of dependence; the dissolution of families; and the material privation of the poor, especially children. Declining caseloads presumably associated with the threat of or actual termination of benefits suggested some decline in dependence. Moynihan acknowledged as much in a posthumously published coauthored paper: "Clearly, welfare reform has been successful in reducing single parents' dependence on social programs alone for economic well-being and in promoting self-reliance through work."[115]

But it is far from clear that welfare reform has in any sense succeeded in alleviating the latter two conditions: family disintegration and poverty. Births to single mothers have continued to rise, and, significantly, they have done so—as Moynihan had long emphasized—across the North Atlantic world,[116] casting serious doubt on the widespread thesis during the 1995 and 1996 debate that withdrawing the supposed economic rewards for nonmarital childbearing would reduce it. Moynihan had rejected the economic determinism implicit in that claim for years, arguing as early as 1973 in *Coping* that "persons who would never dream of having another baby in order to get hold of an additional $8 or $12 a month instantly conclude that, out of depravity, cupidity, ignorance, or whatever, the poor would automatically do so."[117] During the 1996 debate, he characterized the policy under discussion as "an attempt to coerce the poor into behavioral change by deliberately making their lives as wretched as possible. The idea is to make life for the poorest young mothers and their children so utterly miserable that they will not dare bring additional children into the world."[118] He would later invoke this failure of the 1996 repeal to reduce out-of-wedlock births as an instance of the same Rossi's law he had earlier cited as a criticism of Great Society programs.[119] It was simply another utopian attempt to slay poverty with a single shot.

The economic well-being of the poor under welfare reform is harder to gauge. In the posthumous coauthored paper, Moynihan cited "mixed" evidence indicating that "not all who have left welfare have done well economically."[120] More recently, the Census Bureau reported that the child poverty rate was 21.8 percent in 2012, slightly higher than it had been in 1996, and that it had steadily climbed for several years. But with a massive intervening recession, it is difficult to parse causal factors.[121] The question is whether an adequate safety net is still in place to cope with the poverty that remains. Moynihan's most intense fears about repealing the federal entitlement to welfare may not have materialized. But his underlying concerns remain relevant, far from disproved, and captured in the question he raised at the outset of debate on welfare reform in 1995. The issue, he said, was not "the particulars" of policy, but "the principle—the principle. Does the Federal Government maintain a commitment to State programs providing aid to dependent children?"[122]

Reflecting on the episode afterward in his book *Miles to Go,* he evoked Burke: "It is the nature of children to be dependent. The behavior of adults is another matter; but if the two are to be conflated in Washington, it is time, surely, to look elsewhere. . . . It is time for small platoons; a time possibly to be welcomed for such can move quickly, and there are miles to go."[123]

DEFINING DEVIANCY DOWN

During these years and beyond, Moynihan continued to labor against the slow-motion collapse of the American family, which he took to be the one index irrevocably related to poverty. The question was the direction of causation. Early in his career, Moynihan had attributed social disorganization to poverty. Yet a quarter century later, he reflected that the causal arrow actually might point in the other direction. "Why did I write that [social disorganization] was the result of poverty?" he queried. "Why did I not write that poverty was the result of [social disorganization]? Ignorance, as Dr. Johnson observed."[124] But now Moynihan contemplated the possibility that poverty and social disorganization were symbiotic pathologies that fed on one another. Family disintegration was not merely a consequence but also a cause of poverty. Family, for example, was the primary institutional means for the transmission of wealth between generations; conversely, evidence also existed for the "intergenerational transmission of poverty and dependency." As a result, he speculated, "family structure may now be the principal determinant of class structure."[125]

The particular danger was that family dissolution would become so common as to be normalized. This was among the concerns of Moynihan's celebrated essay "Defining Deviancy Down," which appeared in the *American Scholar* in 1993. The essay's generalizations, which have been criticized, reflect the dual perspectives of a scholar seeking insights and a statesman searching for solutions.[126] Building on the work of the sociologist Kai Erikson, Moynihan argued that society could only tolerate a certain amount of deviancy and that once that limit was breached, the society would, rather than suppressing the behaviors in question, simply cease to regard some of them as abnormal. This threshold, he hypothesized, had been crossed. "I proffer the thesis that, over the past generation . . . the amount of deviant behavior in American society has increased beyond the levels the community can 'afford to recognize' and that, accordingly, we have been re-defining deviancy so as to exempt much conduct previously stigmatized."[127] This redefinition took three forms: the "altruistic," such as the emptying of the mental health hospitals in the 1960s; the "opportunistic," which occurred when groups maintained an interest in accepting formerly deviant behavior; and the "normalizing," which he illustrated by reference to the "growing acceptance of unprecedented levels of violent crime."

Interestingly, Moynihan placed the shift in attitudes toward family structure in the second category—the opportunistic—once again evincing his resentment of professionals and interest groups that had stakes in poverty. He wrote: "In this pattern, a growth in deviancy makes possible a transfer of resources, including prestige, to those who control the deviant population. This control would be jeopardized if any serious effort were made to reduce the deviancy in question."[128] It was demonstrably known that the American family was eroding and that a gaping chasm had opened along racial lines. "And yet," he noted, "there is little evidence that these facts are regarded as a calamity in municipal government. To the contrary, there is general acceptance of the situation as normal."[129]

Rather than serious solutions, policy makers offered platitudes and "a fair amount of what could more simply be called dishonesty," such as the oft-repeated claim "Everyone knows that Head Start works."[130] In fact, studies cast serious doubt on that claim, but the money spent on the program was being received by people with a vested interest in retaining it. The case with other education programs was similar, a point on which Moynihan expressed himself bluntly: "*There is good money to be made out of bad schools.* This is a statement that will no doubt please many a hard heart, and displease many genuinely concerned to bring about change. To the latter, a group in which I would like to include myself, I would only say that we are obliged to ask why things do not change."[131]

School textbooks, meanwhile, downplayed the normality of marriage. For its part, a select committee of the House of Representatives produced a fact sheet asserting that the large percentage of children living with single parents was not a new phenomenon. It further noted the decline in the value of welfare benefits to mothers and children, a lament Moynihan shared.

> But no proposal is made to restore benefits to an earlier level, or even to maintain their value. . . . Instead we go directly to the subject of education spending. . . . What is going on here is simply that a large increase in what was once seen as deviancy has provided opportunity to a wide spectrum of interest groups that benefit from re-defining the problem as essentially normal and doing little to reduce it.[132]

Moynihan's third category, the normalization of deviancy, was evident in the declining attention given to violent crime. In Chicago in 1929, he pointed out, "four gangsters killed seven gangsters" in what became known as the St. Valentine's Day Massacre, and "the nation was shocked. . . . It would appear that the society in the 1920s was simply not willing to put up with this degree of deviancy." The Constitution was eventually amended to end Prohibition. Now a similar form of violence had returned due to the narcotics trade but "at a level that induces denial. James Q. Wilson comments that Los Angeles has the equivalent of a St. Valentine's Day Massacre every weekend."[133]

Moynihan concluded his reflections in characteristically prudential, and cautiously optimistic, terms. What he called the "Durkheim constant"—the fixed amount of deviance a society is able to tolerate—fluctuated up and down, he said. Liberals resisted "upward redefining that does injustice to individuals," whereas conservatives "have been correspondingly sensitive to downward redefining that weakens societal standards." Acknowledging that the complexity of society prevented mathematical precision in calculating an appropriate threshold of deviance, he nonetheless asked, "Might it not help if we could all agree that there is a dynamic at work here? It is not a revealed truth, nor yet a scientifically derived formula. It is simply a pattern we observe in ourselves." Made self-aware, "we might surprise ourselves how well we respond to the manifest decline to the American civic order. Might."[134]

Moynihan continued to try. In 1998, just over two years before he retired, he introduced the Enhancing Family Life Act, which was based on James Q. Wilson's ideas. Its proposals included "support[ing] 'second chance' maternity homes for unwed teenage mothers," promoting adoption, and funding early childhood development programs and "a new education assistance program to enable more parents to remain home with young children." The modesty of the proposals is their striking feature, as was Moynihan's hardly flourished rhetorical introduction of them in a press release and statement: "Professor Wilson even quotes the Senator from New York to this effect: 'If you expect a government program to change families, you know more about government than I do.'"[135]

In his last academic work, a posthumously published preface to a collection of conference papers entitled *The Future of the Family*, Moynihan noted that "we are nowhere near a general theory of family change. When such efforts begin, they will give multivariate analysis a whole new meaning."[136] But he was prepared to offer a hypothesis, what he called a "Dahrendorf Inversion." Dahrendorf, again, had said inequality arose from variations in compliance with social norms. But then came the inversion: "Those of unequal rank rise up and change the rules so as to reward their own behavior." Policy makers respond with misdirection, such as the proposed constitutional amendment to define marriage heterosexually ("when all else fails, amend the Constitution").[137] Significantly, though—and aptly for closing a life's reflection on poverty and family—Moynihan ended on an interrogatory note. He observed with apparent approval a seeming return of moral discourse surrounding matters of sex and family, but still he wondered: "Who indeed can tell us what happened to the American family?"[138]

3. The United States in Aspiration

> The Soviet Union is a seriously troubled, even sick society. The indices of economic stagnation and even decline are extraordinary. The indices of social disorder—social pathology is not too strong a term—are even more so. The defining event of the decade might well be the breakup of the Soviet Empire.
>
> —Moynihan, Senate, January 10, 1980

> I was forty before I had any real idea what Burke was about; Kissinger knew in his cradle. On the other hand, I knew what [Woodrow] Wilson was all about.
>
> —Moynihan, *A Dangerous Place*

Editors no longer call press conferences to introduce scholarly essays. But on February 26, 1975, Norman Podhoretz, the chief of *Commentary*, did. The topic was Moynihan's forthcoming article "The United States in Opposition." The *New York Times* previewed it: MOYNIHAN CALLS ON U.S. TO "START RAISING HELL" IN U.N.[1] The *Commentary* article, which landed Moynihan his assignment as US ambassador to the world body, recast the United Nations as a parliamentary system in which anti-Western nations possessed a functioning majority and in which the United States should "go into opposition," utilizing the tool most available to opposition parties—rhetorical combat. The essay reflected his belief that ideas mattered: they had consequences, and the ideological battle being waged against Western liberalism therefore had to be joined, with the United States leading the way for the parliamentary party of liberty.

"The United States in Opposition" forecast Moynihan's combative, controversial tenure at the United Nations, where he had no patience for the bombast of developing nations, especially those sympathetic to the Soviet Union, who blamed Western decadence or exploitation for their internal problems. This tenure marked, in many ways, the beginning of Moynihan's reputation as a neoconservative. And yet, the aide who worked most closely with him during the period, Suzanne Weaver, would later observe that she "signed up for a tour of duty at the UN with Moynihan the neocon—only to see there, in his UN office, a liberal at work, trying assiduously to gain the nonaligned nations' goodwill."[2] The confusion has as much as anything to do with the evolving meanings of the term *neoconservative,* a label that, as noted earlier, Moynihan fiercely rejected. In recent years, it has been associated with a neo-Wilsonian foreign policy that, at least according to critics, is eager to project American force in order to spread American ideals. Whatever the merits or demerits of that position, it was not Moynihan's—not in *Commentary,* not at the United Nations, not as a Scoop Jackson Cold Warrior, and not as a self-professed Wilsonian advocate of international law.

What Moynihan did believe was that the United States needed to engage in a vigorous ideological and political defense of liberty and law in forums where ideological and political battle were done. Yet he had opposed the Vietnam War as early as 1965, even though he both insisted it was an honorable undertaking that was simply a prudential mistake and refused to indulge the self-flagellating rhetoric of the 1960s American Left. In 1979, he criticized President Carter for repeating the charge that the United States had attempted to interfere in the internal affairs of South Vietnam; America had, he insisted, merely tried to repel the communist North. He summarized, "We failed. Very well. Nations often fail. But why describe our failure in terms that make us so culpable rather than merely fallible?"[3] Similarly, he believed the end of the Vietnam War was a reason for national pride rather than shame: "We had brought a war to an end by the withdrawal of political consent to its continuation, as against the withdrawal of constitutional consent, which was the most common sequence elsewhere."[4] The ultimate problem with the war, as he saw it, was not that Americans stood up to communist aggression but rather that the chaos surrounding it became a distraction from that very effort. Moynihan would later reflect that he opposed the war from "a conviction that there existed a growing totalitarian threat to the free nations of the world, and that this threat was becoming ever more menacing as a result of the confusion the Vietnam War was bringing to American perceptions of the nature of that threat."[5]

On those occasions during his Senate career when the use of force was at issue, Moynihan was reticent. He believed the use of force should be bounded by international law, a conviction that was evident as early as the Iran hostage crisis, which began in 1979; the Soviet downing of the civilian Korean Airlines Flight 007 in 1983; and, in the same year, the US invasion of Grenada. Even when international law was used, as in the First Gulf War, Moynihan urged prudence and restraint. He hoped the "new world order" that President George H. W. Bush foresaw emerging in the post-Soviet era would be humanity's second chance to impose a global regime governed by norms of international law.

On foreign policy especially, where Moynihan sat shaped where he stood—or at least how he expressed it. For nearly his entire service in the Senate and even when Democrats were in the majority, Moynihan acted as a needling critic of presidents on foreign policy, a topic on which he must be understood as provocative but also sincere. His perspective from what was often the opposing side both gave him the freedom to goad and required him to do so, with the result that he sometimes occupied the posture of a gadfly. Many of the positions he took, such as criticizing the attempted rescue of the US hostages at the embassy in Tehran (he preferred, as will be seen, that the nation await a ruling from the International Court of Justice) were in line with the stance he assumed at the United Nations: one voice against the crowd.

As always, his knack for creatively reconceptualizing problems enabled unique insights. In foreign policy in particular, Moynihan the senator—never wielding executive responsibility for it—acted more with the freedom of the scholar, injecting new ideas into stale debates. His awareness of the primacy of demographic indicators and ethnic attachments caused him to foresee the Soviet collapse a full decade ahead of the event. He predicted, accurately, that a defining dynamic of the post-

Soviet world would be ethnic conflict. Moynihan's recasting of secrecy as a form of regulation—it regulated what citizens could know rather than what they could do—was the basis of a scorching critique of the self-sustaining secrecy of the security state.

Above all, Moynihan saw America as an aspirational nation. Although his patriotism was never chauvinistic, his pride in the nation's ideals and his confidence in their superiority over totalitarianism were relentless and fierce. He emerged self-consciously from the school of staunchly anticommunist liberalism that despised those elements of the American Left that were in thrall to Stalinism.[6] Just as important, he believed American ideals of themselves could be powerful forces for good in the world. These were the ideals "The United States in Opposition" urged the nation to embrace with a full and unapologetic throat.

"THE UNITED STATES IN OPPOSITION"

The central insight of the *Commentary* essay was that the United Nations operated functionally as a parliament and that, with each nation wielding an equal vote in the General Assembly regardless of population size, the United States in essence led an opposition bloc.[7] The United States and the West more generally were persistent targets of excoriation in global forums, being blamed for the woes of developing nations, accused of exploitation, constantly reminded of the legacy of colonialism, and more. Moynihan's message was clear: raise hell, as he put it, and fight back. In this article and in his subsequent service at the United Nations, he assumed a posture not unlike Burke's in response to the French Revolution: one man standing before the seemingly inevitable tide of history and, in the very name of prudence and armed with ideas, insisting on heroic resistance.

The essay began by excavating the lineage of anti-Americanism as it took hold in developing nations. Membership at the United Nations exploded from 51 states to 138 as the British and other empires dissolved, but, he wrote, "to a quite astonishing degree, [these new countries] were ideologically uniform, having fashioned their polities in terms derived from the general corpus of British socialist opinion as it developed in the period roughly 1890–1950." Moynihan traced much of this relatively mild strain of socialism, which he distinguished from perfervid Soviet communism, to the London School of Economics, where many of the functionaries and future leaders of the nonaligned nations were trained. Its tenets included "a suspicion of, almost a bias against, economic development" and, significantly, anti-Americanism. It was "more anti-American, surely, than it was ever anti-Soviet." British socialism imagined "vast stores of unethically accumulated wealth" piled up by the exploitive West and therefore available for just reclamation by the developing nations. Lastly, he stated, a "distinctive character of the British revolution concerns procedure. Wrongs are to be righted by legislation. The movement was fundamentally parliamentarian."

Moynihan believed it was vital for the West to understand the *ideological* character of its new parliamentary adversary. The United States had "not seen the ideology as distinctive" and therefore had been unable to deal with it. Totalitarian states, which trucked in ideologies, recognized it more easily, and even though it became clear that the Third World was not going to align explicitly with the communists, the Soviets saw they could nonetheless divide this group from the West. The Third World bloc persistently attacked the West in political and ideological forums, often with flagrant hypocrisy—such as charging the United States with violating civil liberties while political prisoners languished in the accusers' own jails—and the West persistently declined to defend itself. Sometimes, the United States even voted for resolutions hostile to its own interests. Granted, the acts of bodies such as the General Assembly and other forums in which the remnants of the former empires held sway were of "limited force," he remarked, but

> so [were] the pronouncements of the Continental Congress. They are not on that ground to be ignored. What then does the United States do?
>
> *The United States goes into opposition.* This is our circumstance.

We are a minority. We are outvoted. This is neither an unprecedented nor an intolerable situation. The question is what do we make of it. So far we have made little—nothing—of what in fact is an opportunity.

Going into opposition meant engaging critics of the West on rhetorical and political grounds—three in particular. First, the United States should proudly defend liberalism. Radicalism had brought about "an exceptional deprecation of the achievements of liberal processes," and these achievements had to be recovered and defended. "The truth is that international liberalism and its processes have enormous recent achievements to their credit," he declared. "It is time for the United States to start saying so."

Second, the United States should not accept a false stipulation of economic crisis used to justify radical demands. Doing so would, he acknowledged, "require a considerable shift in the government mind, and possibly even some movement in American elite opinion also, for we have become great producers and distributors of crisis." Any crisis the United States attempted to resolve in an international forum was likely to be decided against its interests—"Ergo: skepticism, challenge." Certainly, the free economies were performing better than their socialist counterparts, which were focused on redistribution rather than production.[8] "It is a good argument," he said. "Far better, surely, than the repeated plea of *nolo contendere* which we have entered, standing accused before the body of the people."

Third, the United States needed to start speaking frankly about the condition of civil liberties in Western societies compared to those of the nations attacking them. "It is time . . . that the American spokesman came to be feared in international forums for the truths he might tell," Moynihan asserted. The United States behaved aggressively at the UN Security Council but had become "extraordinarily passive" on this topic in other UN forums. Consequently, he said, "it is past time we ceased to apologize for an imperfect democracy. Find its equal. It is time we grew out of our—not a little condescending—supersensitivity about the feelings of new nations. It is time we commenced to treat them as equals, a respect to which they are entitled." The Third World had a "constitutional heritage of individual liberty" that it should be encouraged to prize, as, for example, India had. But American diplomats should not be supine in the face of attacks on the issue of political freedom from regimes with atrocious civil liberties records. This was especially true in the age-old debate between liberty and equality. Recalling an Israeli socialist who had said nations that valued liberty over equality had achieved more equality than those who valued equality over liberty, Moynihan declared: "*This is our case.* We are of the liberty party, and it might surprise us what energies might be released were we to unfurl those banners."

At the United Nations, he did, to both acclaim and accusation. When Idi Amin, the lunatic dictator of Uganda, delivered a tirade to the United Nations denouncing Israel and the United States, Moynihan, eschewing the State Department's preference for appeasing Africa, responded forcefully. In a speech to the staunchly anticommunist American Federation of Labor and Congress of Industrial Organizations (AFL-CIO), he said the United States wanted to participate in economic progress for the developing world. "It must be clear, however," he added, "that the United States doesn't wish to do this because we accept responsibility for the economic condition of the Third and Fourth Worlds. We repudiate the charge that we have exploited or plundered other countries." The United States, he continued, prized "the primacy of the individual—the rights of the individual, the welfare of the individual, the claims of the individual against those of the state."[9] A diplomatic uproar resulted, and Moynihan was accused of insulting Africa. By the next Monday morning, the staff at the US mission to the United Nations had prepared "an explanatory press release," seeking to calm tensions by saying that "some of Amin's statements before the General Assembly earned wide approval: others were morally offensive." Moynihan would recall: "I let it be known that not one goddamn thing Amin had said had won my 'wide approval.'"[10]

When the Zionism-as-racism resolution began to take shape,

Moynihan reflected, it was concern about its Soviet origins and Western-bashing overtones rather than affinity for the Jewish state (though that would develop) that initially moved him. He remarked of the resolution, "It reeked of the totalitarian mind, stank of the totalitarian state."[11] Yet Western societies faced nearly insuperable psychological difficulties responding to accusations from illiberal societies.

> There is probably not now in the whole of the world a totalitarian
> state which does not have a constitution guaranteeing individual
> liberties. On the other hand, there is not a liberal society which does
> not contain a real Marxist or neo-Marxist movement dedicated to
> its overthrow on grounds of insufficient liberality. Nor is there any
> liberal society which is not torn by doubts on this score. Yeats
> sensed the mood:
>> Come fix upon me that accusing eye.
>> I thirst for accusation . . . [12]

Latent in Moynihan's defense of the West was a defense of national particularity. Although he believed in a liberal regime of international law, he also believed in national borders and identities. Moynihan rejected "a universal society" in favor of one with borders. This, he said, might be the basis of security, "for a particular society is a society that can be defended, and, I think, will be."[13]

Late in Moynihan's tenure at the United Nations, tensions with Secretary of State Henry Kissinger—who would have preferred a less assertive stance at the world body—approached a breaking point. The contours of Moynihan's reaction are crucial for understanding the hawkish character of his early Senate rhetoric. Observe the contrast he drew between Kissinger's realism and his own apparent Wilsonian idealism: "I was forty before I had any real idea what Burke was about; Kissinger knew in his cradle. On the other hand, I knew what Wilson was all about. I knew what Rebecca West had written of Versailles, that to the new nations it was deliverance."[14] Kissinger, of course, was not a Burkean properly speaking. Burke's heroic and principled resistance to the French Revolution lay outside the contours of a realism that simply gives in to circumstances as one finds them. But Burke certainly would have rejected the open-ended abstract idealism of a Wilsonian claim such as self-determination.

For Moynihan, the right of new nations to self-determination was "a tie we had, a claim we had, that could be put to our purposes." He cited as an example Kissinger's lack of substantive reaction to Soviet attempts to infiltrate the Lebanese government. Moynihan acknowledged that his desire for a muscular reaction could be read as hawkish, "as if, were the choice mine, I would have been sending carriers into the eastern Mediterranean. I would not have." He had, he recalled, opposed Vietnam, and he was in no mood for a repeat. "But I wanted us to show our colors even so, to argue back. This is a form of resistance, even of offensive. It is not the least dangerous weapon a nation can wield."[15] Vietnam had been a mistake because the United States could not "halt a totalitarian advance there—not at costs acceptable to a liberal society. But . . . if anything, it added enormously to the importance of *ideological* resistance."[16]

The point—and it distinguishes Moynihan especially from contemporary neoconservatism—is that he wanted to wage *ideological* warfare in *ideological* forums. He was confident ideas of themselves would be felt, would make an imprint on the world. This commitment does connect him with the first wave of neoconservative thinkers, among them Irving Kristol, who emphasized ideological resistance—if not with a later wave that would emphasize the military dimensions of the same ideals. For his part, Moynihan was willing to use military strength to *defend* freedom, but he counseled prudence in efforts to *expand* it. The nature of his Wilsonianism was rooted in ideas rather than arms. His Wilson was a juridical rather than a crusading figure. Force was to be extended through the medium of international law.

Moynihan did, however, believe US military posture was connected to ideas in two pivotal ways. First, military presence was connected to political influence. His concern, though the details remain somewhat obscure, was that a posture of weakness would not merely encourage

Soviet expansionism but also, perhaps more damaging, inhibit the American capacity for political resistance to Soviet mischief. Perception seems to have been key here: relative weakness of arms meant relative weakness of influence. Second, America's moral superiority over the Soviet Union in the nuclear arms race depended on the capacity of its nuclear arsenal to sustain a first strike. The nation could thus plausibly insist it had no intention of launching nuclear weapons except in response to a Soviet attack; first strikes were the business of the Soviets alone. Moynihan would, for this reason, spend the first period of his Senate career raising strong concerns about the weakening of the US nuclear posture—a position he later appeared to suggest was mistaken.

THE SENATOR AND THE SOVIETS

Moynihan's maiden Senate speech opposed the nomination of the diplomat Paul Warnke to head the Arms Control and Disarmament Agency. Warnke's article "Apes on a Treadmill" characterized the United States and the Soviet Union as mimicking one another, driving pointless and endless increases in nuclear arsenals.[17] The United States, Warnke argued, should stop in the hope the Soviets would reciprocate. Moynihan was having none of it, especially what he took to be Warnke's moral equivalence between the Cold War adversaries. He warned of a perception of American decline—indeed, a decline of liberalism generally in a world "in which there are barely three dozen democratic societies left alive." The Soviet Union had assumed an aggressive stance, and the nuclear arms race reflected not apish imitation but rather "an expression of fundamentally differing goals, basic conflict and a growing disparity of condition." American military power had been created and had to be maintained "because we face a determined and powerful foe who will exploit our weaknesses to advance interests adverse to ours and political beliefs we find abhorrent."[18]

In 1977—when President Carter gave a commencement address at Notre Dame announcing the nation's new freedom from its "inordinate fear of communism" and suggesting the great new global divide was not between the enslaved and free nations of the East and West but rather between the prosperous and poor of the North and South—Moynihan responded with a commencement address of his own, this one at Baruch College in New York City. "The President leads where I for one would not wish to follow," he declared, denying that "we should divert our attention from the central political struggle of our time—that between liberal democracy and totalitarian Communism—and focus instead on something else." The North-South divide deserved attention, but so did what Michael Novak had called the "significantly growing imperial power of the Soviet Union." Genuine care for the developing world had to be manifested in equal concern about Soviet expansionism, which, Moynihan emphasized, threatened developing nations most of all.[19]

As late as March 1979, he was still arguing that "totalitarianism was expanding as a principle of social organization and growing more powerful as it did so. . . . Things would get worse before they would get better." The belief that the Soviets would respond in kind to unilateral reductions in American arms reflected a "flight from reality." Even in this period, though, Moynihan was still emphasizing a political and ideological rather than a militaristic defense of national interests. It was necessary, he stressed, to convince the Soviets to reduce nuclear arms— "theirs far more than ours"—but also to "persuad[e] them that we are no longer in thrall to any notion that it is our too-great power that is the true cause of instability in the world."[20] What was required was not simply to accumulate more weaponry but rather to maintain the US capacity to withstand a Soviet first strike and thus both a credible deterrent and a morally superior position.[21]

Yet by late that year, Moynihan's assessment of the Soviet threat began to shift. He now saw the Soviet Union as a decrepit, failing society. What most impressed him, he later said, was data indicating that "contrary you might say to all possibility, infant mortality in the Soviet Union was going up, and the life expectancy of males was going down. Demography is destiny, and there was the future of Soviet society for all to see."[22] The defection of Arkady N. Shevchenko, the high-ranking Soviet diplomat, during Moynihan's tenure at the United Nations had also influenced him. Significantly, it was not merely demography but also ideology that caught his attention: Shevchenko "described in detail a police state in which political belief had all but leached out of the system."[23] But in truth, the seeds of doubt appear to have been planted early. Moynihan had heard it from the antiutopian Oakeshott at the London School of Economics. A Burkean ethic of limitation was in the background:

> And so for many of us the specter of world communism, as it was then termed, never seemed in any way as imminent, as urgent as it did to much of Western opinion. A man like Oakeshott introduced you to the idea of the futility of overreaching. The Bible does much the same. Armed with that idea, it was possible to examine the reality of the communist "experiment" and anticipate the inevitability of its failure.[24]

By late 1979, Moynihan had reached a stunning conclusion: Soviet society was not only decaying, it was dying, and it was not only dying, it was doomed in the relatively near term. That November, *Newsweek* asked several leading thinkers to make predictions for the 1980s. The prescience of Moynihan's response, Godfrey Hodgson wrote, was "eerie": "The Soviet empire is coming under tremendous strain. It could blow up. The world could blow up with it." Moreover, in addition to seeing the end, Moynihan forecast its terms. The Soviet Union would break apart along ethnic lines: "Now the nationality strains begin. Whatever Marxism may have meant to intellectuals, it is ethnic identity that has stirred the masses of the twentieth century, and they are stirring near the Russian borders." But Moynihan was not for that reason either dovish or triumphalist. "Good news?" he asked. "Hardly. The problem is that the internal weaknesses of the Soviet Union have begun to appear at the moment when its external strength has never been greater."[25] The Soviet bear might begin to act like a wounded one—aggressively.

As if to vindicate Moynihan's fears, the Soviets invaded Afghanistan the next month. Thereupon, to Moynihan's approval, President Carter pulled the SALT II Treaty from Senate consideration. In January 1980, Moynihan inserted a lengthy reflection into the *Congressional Record* on the significance of the moment. The Carter administration had finally taken a tough political stand against the Soviets. Yet the West also had to understand that American power had declined, not least because of the domestic mind-set that blamed global instability on American dominance. That was not to say the United States should retreat to the bearing of apology he had so criticized in "The United States in Opposition." Ideological force remained key, "for the power of the United States rests upon and derives from the ideas we represent: in international affairs from the standards of conduct which we aver and which we seek to uphold." Still, prudence was in order. Moynihan seemed to have himself in mind as he said, "It will be both the irony and the gravest reality of the time now ahead that the counsel of restraint in foreign affairs must come from those who have been depicted in the recent past as somehow the most bellicose."

What the United States needed, he reflected, were principles backed up by policy. It had had principles without policy, and now—as the administration turned to totalitarian China for help in resisting the Soviet invasion of Afghanistan—the situation seemed to have flipped. The key was to recognize the power of ideas. "The object of policy," he said, "is to make one's nation understood." For seventy years, the Soviets had done so: their foreign policy was obviously driven by a principle—the success of the global Marxist-Leninist project—and everyone knew it. The United States needed to be as forceful in defending *its* ideals.

At the same time, American leaders also needed to apprehend the Soviet threat accurately. Moynihan recalled his 1977 exchange of commencement addresses with Carter. Of his own speech, he said he "would not much change those words today, but I would add to them the complexity to which I have alluded": "The Soviet Union is a seriously troubled, even sick society. The indices of economic stagnation and even decline are extraordinary. The indices of social disorder—social pathology is not too strong a term—are even more so. The defining event of the decade might well be the break-up of the Soviet Empire. But that . . . could also be the defining danger of the decade." This was a moment for an "ordinate fear of communism." The significance of Afghanistan was that the Soviets in their desperation were executing a "pincer movement" around the oil fields of the Persian Gulf. Moynihan called on the administration to deploy the necessary arms and troops to the region to make clear the United States would resist any Soviet attempt to seize the gulf's oil supplies.[26]

Yet Moynihan's own fear of communism began to ease as the Soviet Union grew more internally unsustainable. Accordingly, Michael Barone wrote, "Moynihan began voting with the foreign policy doves but for different reasons: They believed that the Soviet Union was dangerous but not evil, that we should mollify it and try to downsize both sides' military forces; Moynihan believed that the Soviet Union was evil but not dangerous, and so the military buildup of the 1980s was largely unnecessary."[27]

Moynihan would later describe himself as having "quite changed my mind. I had grown convinced that the danger from the Soviet Union would not come from its expansion, but its disintegration."[28] During this period, he resisted the Reagan administration's MX missile as a first-strike weapon that upended the policy of deterrence. In May 1984, delivering a commencement address at New York University, he announced what amounted to an elemental reassessment. American policy was now encouraging a Soviet nuclear buildup with "no conceivable military purpose," only political ones. The heightened tensions distressed him. Meanwhile, the United States was abandoning the basic pillars of the post–World War II international order: international law, nuclear deterrence, and the quest for arms control. "But somehow, of late," he stated, "we seem to be mistaking [the postwar order] for a sign of weakness, and attributing that weakness to the rise of Soviet strength. What pitiful stuff that is. The truth is that the Soviet idea is spent. It commands some influence in the world; and fear. But it summons no loyalty. History is moving away from it with astounding speed." The global challenges confronting the nation were changing, including—and here, again, he was prescient—terrorism and tribalism that attacked modernity itself. "Are these not challenges enough for one generation?" he asked. "I suggest they are, and I offer a closing thought: our grand strategy should be to wait out the Soviet Union; its time is passing. Let us resolve to be here, our old selves, with an ever surging font of ideas. When the time comes, it will be clear that in the end freedom did prevail."[29]

When the collapse came, the question was what would happen next. Moynihan hoped the post-Soviet era would usher in a resurgence of international law as the basis for the relations between states. To see why, we must explore his complicated intellectual relationship with the ideas of a man he esteemed—but about whom he maintained no illusions: Woodrow Wilson.

"WAS WOODROW WILSON RIGHT?"[30]

On Moynihan's reading, Wilson was responsible for projecting two ideals into the twentieth century: national self-determination and international law. We shall return to the first—an ideal Moynihan admired even as he acknowledged its difficulties—in discussing his reflections on ethnicity in international affairs. It is the second, grounding the behavior and relations of states in the law of nations, that concerns us now. Moynihan's belief in international law has led critics to charge that he changed his mind, with the bellicosity of his UN years giving way to a desire to restrain America's conduct with a harness its Soviet adversary refused to wear. Moynihan would not have regarded a charge that he changed his mind in response to changing circumstances as an epithet, but in this case, that did not occur. His endorsement of international law actually preceded his tenure at the United Nations; in fact, it formed the basis of his belief that the United States should oppose totalitarianism forthrightly. Equally important, his understanding of international law was hardly pacifist. He believed that its efficacy depended on enforcement and that its utility might often justify the use of military might.

In 1974, during his service as ambassador to India, Moynihan was invited to give a lecture at the Woodrow Wilson Center for International Scholars. The occasion was the fiftieth anniversary of Wilson's death, and Moynihan undertook to rehabilitate the late president's reputation against a persistent assumption that his idealism was ill suited to the complexities and dangers of the post–Cold War world. Moynihan acknowledged Wilson's flaws frankly, admitting that the president could be sanctimonious, arrogant, and manipulative. He also related one anecdote about Wilson meeting a group of Azerbaijanis. The president said he had not theretofore heard of their country, but he nonetheless concluded that they spoke the same language of ideas, liberty, rights, and justice that he did. Wilson could not possibly have believed this, Moynihan reflected. "Worse: What if indeed he did?" he asked. Even more troubling for a new generation of Americans, he continued, was Wilson's claim that the Azerbaijanis were turning to the United States for salvation.[31]

Moynihan argued that Wilson's ideas had to be grasped through an understanding of his view of humanity. "Wilson's vision of a world order," he said, "was a religious vision: of the natural goodness of man prevailing through the Holy Ghost of Reason." Yet this vision arose from religious assumptions that, though still held privately by individuals, were "no longer seen to imply political belief as well,"[32] seemingly calling into question their continuing applicability. Moreover, because Wilson's quest for a legalistic world order failed to prevent the subsequent atrocities of the twentieth century, "events increasingly persuade us to act as if Wilson were wrong."[33] But there was, Moynihan would later reflect, no alternative to Wilson's vision of international law other than the raw exercise of force—in the formulation of William Wordsworth that Moynihan often quoted, "The good old rule / the simple plan / that they should take who have the power / and they should keep who can."[34] Even the Athenian side in the Melian Dialogue, he once wryly observed, appealed to precedent: "It is not as if we were the first to make this law [that the strong do what they can and the weak suffer what they must], or act upon it when made: we found it existing before us, and shall leave it to exist forever after us."[35]

A difficulty nonetheless presents itself—not for Moynihan per se but for the thesis of this book. To the extent Moynihan was a Wilsonian, can he also be called a Burkean? That is, can Wilson's idealistic hopes be squared with Burke's grounded prudence as a principle of international relations? Part of the answer lies in caricaturing neither Burke nor, as will presently be seen (at least on Moynihan's account), Wilson. Burke did frequently acknowledge—indeed, invoke—the authority of international law, which he called "the great ligament of mankind."[36] He believed the principles of the "law of nations" vindicated British resistance to the French Revolution and American discontent with parliamentary taxation. And they condemned the British governor-general Warren Hastings's abuses in India.

As Peter Stanlis has written, international law for Burke was not an abstraction, nor did it replace the particularity of political communities; instead, it formed "a new, hypothetical, transitional law between the universal natural law and the particular constitutions of particular states."[37] Prudence struck the balance between them.[38] Though, again, no particular influence of Burke on Moynihan is asserted here, the compatibility between the ideas of the two men is striking. For Moynihan, international law *was* a prudential means of grounding and judging the behavior of nations. He thus rejected the association of international law with the airy romanticism of a Thomas Paine or Walt Whitman as opposed to the hardheaded realism of an Edmund Burke or James Madison; the real case, he insisted, was the other way around.[39]

Moynihan took this to be Wilson's position as well—a point obscured by the vulgarization of Wilsonianism in its invocation in contemporary politics as a synonym for an aggressive strain of neoconservative foreign policy. If anything, it was the purported realists who spoke in romanticized terms: "Indeed," Moynihan wrote, "in the great game of semantic infiltration, to employ Fred Iklé's marvelous term, there has been no greater success than that of the nineteenth-century romantics who, in the foreign policy debates of twentieth-century America, got their adversaries to call them realists."[40] This was obscured by a confusion of Wilsonianism with "soft moralism"—the proclamation "of ideals that were unenforceable," such as the 1928 Kellogg-Briand Pact outlawing war. Moynihan distinguished moralism from morality, noting that the former represented a flight from responsibility whereas the latter was grounded in it. Moralism confused the domestic terms of political debate with the imperatives of the international realm, in which a state's first responsibility is "peace and security." The realism of Wilson's vision was further blurred by the generation of self-described realists, such as George Kennan, who associated Wilsonianism with naive idealism—"the prattle," as Moynihan paraphrased this view, "of soft and privileged people in a hard and threatening world." The failures of Vietnam seemed to confirm this view, resulting in "neo-isolationism."[41]

"But this," Moynihan continued in the 1974 address, "was a corruption of Wilson." Wilson's achievement had been to define patriotism in terms amenable to the contemporary American condition, which was bound up with global leadership. This patriotism meant "the duty to defend and, where feasible, to advance democratic principles in the world at large." Here, Moynihan stepped explicitly beyond the boundaries of prudence: patriotism entailed the duty "always to defend [democratic principles]—prudently if possible, but at the risk, if need be, of imprudence." Yet his limitation of this imprudence to the *defense* of freedom where it existed—a narrowing sphere in the heyday of Soviet expansionism—itself adds an element of prudence that distinguishes Moynihan from neoconservatives who would later speak in terms of the active enlargement of democratic ideals.

This understanding of patriotism came to Wilson—"Scotch-Irish, his father a Presbyterian minister, his mother a Presbyterian minister's daughter, in whom, Richard Hofstadter wrote, the Calvinist spirit burned with a bright and imperishable flame"—with intellectual ease. But elites no longer held such views, Moynihan remarked, "and in the absence of religious conviction, it is not possible to establish an obligation of the Wilsonian kind to the state."[42] Still, Americans retained "a sense of justice and procedure, a feeling for law, which is wholly service-able as a belief system around which to organize a national life."[43]

The difficulty lay in Wilson's apparent fervor for patriotism as, in the president's words, "a principle of action.... Every man should be careful to have an available surplus of energy over and above what he spends upon himself and his own interests, to spend for the advancement of his neighbors, of his people, of his nation." For Moynihan, ever the devotee of subsidiarity, this required the navigation of a middle course through Wilson, for "the specter of statism hovers about such words.... It always will, when attachment to the state rather than mere submission is pro-posed." But the state could still serve as "an extension of the moral force and responsibility of the individual." He continued, "This at least is not moralism. It does not discover virtue in weakness. It argues, rather, the unique and necessary virtue of strength, of men and women becoming all they are capable of being, beyond anything accorded to them in the past." Moynihan acknowledged the twentieth century's awful history with the state "submerg[ing] the individual in the mass." But attempt-ing, perhaps too hard, to rehabilitate Wilson from the very statism he had just identified, he asserted that the president "argue[d] the elevation of the individual, the differentiation of each. It may be more than we can do: but this very thought, so much a product of the events that fol-lowed Wilson, is the essential case for trying."[44]

The contemporary context of Wilsonianism lay in "the worldwide struggle between free societies and those not free."[45] This assertion—more than a year before "The United States in Opposition" appeared and before Moynihan's tenure at the United Nations—refutes charges that Moynihan subsequently discovered international law and went soft. His resignation from the United Nations, he wrote, resulted from an ex-tended disagreement between his Wilsonianism and Kissinger's pur-ported realism. For Kissinger, "what had Woodrow Wilson signified to the Europe in which Kissinger was born save a peace treaty that led di-rectly to another war, and a doctrine of self-determination that aroused ethnic passions to the point where his own people, the Jews of Germany, were all but destroyed?"[46] For Moynihan, by contrast, it was Wilsonian ideals that legitimated US resistance to totalitarianism.

They might also have helped to resolve a coming difficulty in domestic American politics. The multiethnic character of American society—a phenomenon, incidentally, "for which [Wilson] had no little distaste"— meant any struggle for personal liberty or self-determination anywhere in the world would affect domestic politics because domestic ethnic groups would favor their own nationalities. The United States needed an objective principle by which to resolve these disputes. It ought to be liberty but—as in Stanlis's understanding of Burke—liberty leavened by prudence:

> I would argue that there is only one course likely to make the internal strains of [domestic ethnic] conflicts [related to international affairs] endurable, and that is for the United States deliberately and consistently to bring its influence to bear on behalf of those regimes which promise the largest degree of personal and national liberty. We shall have to do so with prudence, with care. We are granted no license to go looking for trouble, no right to meddle. We shall have to continue to put up with obnoxious things about which there is nothing we can do; and often we may have to restrain ourselves where there are things we can do. Yet we must play the hand dealt us: we stand for liberty, for the expansion of liberty. Anything less risks the contraction of liberty: our own included.[47]

Moynihan wrote in *A Dangerous Place* that he later realized this passage amounted to a view of Kissinger's realism: "I realized finally that he saw us as a deracinated people, who had lost our political faith much as the English, earlier, had lost their religious belief and 'wandered into nothingness.' I was not ready to settle for this." He took his view to be liberal, that is, situated in the long tradition of "liberal internationalism."

Yet Moynihan's view of Wilson was not hagiographic. He hinted several times that he believed American participation in World War I was unnecessary—motivated as much by Wilson's personal Anglophilia,

rooted in his own ethnic attachments, as by any ethical or legal principle. Intriguingly, he also wrote that "step by step, Wilson took the nation
into war on grounds that international law left no recourse,"[48] a formulation that, to the extent the war was unnecessary, suggests international
law can be put to ill purposes as well as good ones. He blamed Wilson's
imperiousness and inflexibility for the failure of the League of Nations.
He said Wilson's diplomacy became "messianic."[49] Moynihan wrote that
the idea of national self-determination, though a triumph that revolu-
tionized how the world gauges the legitimacy of states, was also half-
baked in key respects, unleashing expectations that contributed to the
ethnic conflict of the twentieth century.

Still, all told, he concluded, Wilson's hopes were—if idealistic—better
than the alternatives: "Granted, the repeated invocation of international
law partook . . . of the dottiness of nineteenth-century enthusiasms, and
of the sanctimoniousness. . . . And yet, was it wrong for these Americans
to approach the twentieth century concerned to uphold these standards
which might be lost? Was Woodrow Wilson wrong to think there might
be something better ahead than Auschwitz and Hiroshima? Absurd? Yes,
at times absurd."[50]

THE LAW OF NATIONS

Vietnam imposed many costs on the political order, Moynihan believed.
One of them was "a great falling off of confidence" in normative standards such as the universal applicability of liberal democracy. He wrote,
"In sum: Wilsonian thinking had already got us into sufficient trouble;
it could only get us into worse."[51] As a result, by the time Moynihan arrived in the Senate, he felt international law was no longer honored, or
even much remembered, as a basis for international relations. The problem was that its abandonment by the United States licensed a similar
abandonment by others. If America was free to act wherever its interests
were at stake, he argued, were not the Soviets as well? Moynihan freely
granted that the Soviets routinely violated international law. What he

rejected was the idea that this relieved the United States of its responsibilities. ("If one is prepared to have the Soviet Union set standards of conduct for the United States, well and good.")[52] Similarly, Moynihan once pointed out the irony, if not outright hypocrisy—he rather politely called it an "opposed tendency"—of President Reagan condemning the hijacking of TWA Flight 847 by invoking international law in a speech before the American Bar Association at the precise moment his administration was urging that organization to reject a resolution describing international law as binding on the United States.[53]

Moynihan's acquaintance with the subject marks one of his earliest interests and commitments. His doctoral dissertation at Tufts University detailed the emergence of US participation in the International Labor Organization. Significantly, he described the movement for international labor standards as "conservative, practical and easy to understand." Its conservatism sounds Burkean: "In essence the idea of international labor legislation is one of reform as against revolution. It proceeds from the assumption of the legitimacy of the capitalist concern with competition." Its practicality lay in the need for shared labor standards to secure a level playing field for trade.[54]

International law, to Moynihan, continued to be pragmatic. It could serve to organize American initiatives, assemble support, and license the use of force. Conversely, US violations—such as the US military's forcible search of the Nicaraguan embassy in Panama in pursuit of the fugitive dictator Manuel Noriega in 1990—made it more difficult to oppose violations by others, including the Iraqi intrusions on foreign embassies in Kuwait later that year.[55]

International law might have legitimated the use of force, he argued, during the Iran hostage crisis of 1979 and 1980. His reaction to the Carter administration's unsuccessful rescue mission shows how far—perhaps too far—he took the commitment. The US protest of the Iranian seizure of the Tehran embassy was pending a final ruling—a favorable interim one had already been issued—from the International Court of Justice when the rescue was attempted. By acting in advance of it, the administration gave the Soviet judge on the panel the cover he needed subsequently to vote against the United States, whereas patience, Moynihan asserted, would have produced a unanimous decision that would have legitimated wholesale, if unsurprising, force: "Quite possibly some or all of the hostages would have died. Vastly greater numbers died to put in place the principles we would now be defending. . . . If need be, fire and sword to the gates of Teheran. What was the matter with that? 'The firm foundation of government,' Woodrow Wilson often said, 'is not pity but justice.'"[56]

The Reagan administration was even blunter in its rejection of international law as a standard. "The idea of international law had faded," Moynihan wrote. "But just as important, in the 1980s it had come to be associated with weakness in foreign policy. Real men did not cite Grotius."[57] One early result was what Moynihan regarded as the illegal US invasion of Grenada following a communist coup in 1983. The invasion, he argued, violated the charters of the United Nations and the Organization of American States; if an Arab nation similarly invaded Israel, the United States had forfeited its moral right to protest at law.[58] The proper response to the communist coup, Moynihan believed, was a letter of condolence. The United States would still be available for assistance in cases of natural disaster, but at the first crop failure, the Grenadians "would have to look to Moscow and learn the joys of the bear's embrace."[59]

Instead, the new "realist" view saw international law as literally unreal because it was not backed by the same kind of enforcement system as domestic law. "Yet neither [was] most domestic law for most of history. . . . Many a system of law depends on self-enforcement. . . . Law is confused with force."[60] International law had been seen as binding for all of American history until the twentieth century, when "the law-abiding emerged as victims."[61] The resulting idea that the violations of other nations released the United States from its own obligations was, Moynihan insisted, wholly new. "If the Soviets 'renounce' international law by, let us say, invading Afghanistan, the United States is not free to respond by invading Grenada."[62]

Nor was the CIA free to mine the harbors of communist Nicaragua to discourage its interference with neighboring El Salvador, as the agency did in 1983. Moynihan, who was vice chairman of the Senate Select Committee on Intelligence at the time, condemned the move sternly. This is not to say he was soft on totalitarianism in Managua. In fact, he described Nicaraguan interference in Salvadoran affairs as itself a violation of international law, and he had successfully sought funding for intelligence activities against Nicaragua for three years.[63] But he said his purpose in doing so was to *uphold* international law. By contrast, the mining was an act of war; the United States had handed a totalitarian state a victory before international legal tribunals, from which the Reagan administration escaped only by arbitrarily declaring it would not recognize the World Court's jurisdiction with respect to Central American affairs for a period of two years.

In a news conference, President Reagan defended a nation's right to engage in covert activity like the mining "when it believes that its interests are best served." Moynihan zeroed in on the claim as legitimating any behavior by any state, anytime, anywhere: Reagan was essentially saying a nation could do whatever it wanted. "This . . . is a wholly normless statement," Moynihan insisted. "A nation has such a right if it is *in* the right—which is to say, if its behavior is consonant with international law." The mitigating role of Burkean prudence in the law of nations was evident as he added: "I speak of that institutional state of mind which, having lost the principle of proportionality basic to all law, can think of no option as between doing nothing, or next to nothing, and blowing up the world."[64] It was no coincidence to him that, international law having been forsaken, domestic law was put to the curb next. Congress reacted to the mining by cutting off funding to the Nicaraguan contras, and the Iran contra affair ensued: "The whole setting was normless to the point of nihilism. The plain fact is that the president did invite and almost certainly did deserve impeachment."[65]

The fundamental mistake critics of international law made, Moynihan argued, was in concluding its only purpose was restraint. In fact, properly understood, it was a tool for legitimating force. This was basic to the idea of law itself. Moynihan thus offered the hypothesis that "[a] political culture from which the idea of international law has largely disappeared places its initiatives in jeopardy." Treaties were a means of exerting leverage when force was necessary. "International law is not a scheme for surrender; it is not a unilateral, self-imposed restriction on the law-abiding; it is not a suicide pact. To the contrary, where relevant, it is a framework for deciding how and when to use force. It is correspondingly a mode of marshaling support."[66]

That was precisely the case when international law was suddenly reasserted in the global reaction to Iraq's 1990 invasion of Kuwait. The Soviet Union was in its death throes; this was the end of the "Twentieth Century War" that had begun with the Paris Peace Conference—touching off a decades-long struggle between the visions of Wilson (the law of nations), on the one hand, and Lenin (the law of history), on the other.[67] In 1988, Soviet chairman Mikhail Gorbachev had stunned the world by invoking the Latin maxim "*pacta sunt servanda*"—agreements must be honored—before the United Nations. "The chairman of the Presidium of the Supreme Soviet had come to New York," Moynihan would later reflect, "and offered terms of surrender."[68] Moynihan instantly saw both the imperative and the opportunity. The day Iraq invaded, he asked on the Senate floor: "Might we now return to the idea that *law* is at issue here? In the coming days many will denounce Saddam Hussein for his 'immoral' behavior. Immoral it is, but more importantly he has committed a crime."[69] It did not help that the United States had turned a blind eye to Hussein's prior violations of the law of nations, such as his uses of chemical weapons. But the invasion of Kuwait triggered "the sudden emergence of 'the rule of law' as the lodestar of American foreign policy."[70] That summer, he said, "the President of the United States took to invoking 'international law,' the 'rule of law,' and Chapter VII of the United Nations Charter, as if such terms were part of the working vocabulary of American statecraft. In fact, they had all but disappeared."[71]

Moynihan interpreted this as a transformation in American views—a welcome one, to be sure, but a transformation nonetheless. He described it in Burkean terms. Circumstance rather than abstraction was now regnant: "The terrible reign of doctrine was over once again: information regained some of its authority, in foreign affairs at all events. As information is more difficult to come by than ideas, foreign policy became cautious once again."[72] This rediscovery of international law was to be welcomed, and though this change ought to have been acknowledged, it did not need to be accompanied by an apology. "To the contrary," Moynihan said, "we are never more ourselves than when we return to the roots of American conviction."[73]

However, he then surprised many observers by voting against authorization for the Gulf War—a vote that, Godfrey Hodgson wrote (without explanation), was the one Moynihan most regretted from his Senate career.[74] The reason for his vote appears to have been prudential. Despite his invocation of international law, Moynihan accused Bush of resorting to the absolutist typologies of the Cold War, as in the president's statement that "no price is too heavy to pay" for standing up to Iraqi aggression. Again channeling the Burkean rejection of extremes (but perhaps with overwrought rhetoric—something also not entirely foreign to Burke), Moynihan asked what "possesse[d] the President to declare" such a thing.

> No price? Five million Arab casualties, for example? Conflagration in the Middle East? The exhaustion of American military resources? It is enough simply to ask the question to realize the answer. The answer being that we are prepared and ought to be prepared to pay *some* price, but not *any* price. The problem is that the Cold War mode of decision making does not admit of such proportionality. Or does not do so readily.[75]

On the eve of the war, Moynihan once again emphasized proportionality. After the Cold War, he observed, "a certain normality reappears. Which is to say a sense of proportion. Why should this not now phase over into a sense of proportion about what is at stake in the Gulf? Important principles, yes. Ultimate issues, no."[76] In Senate debate, he insisted the relevant American interest lay in reestablishing a regime of international law—a goal that, he asserted, war at that point would not attain. His reasoning here was, at best, obscure. He stated that "the international community has not yet agreed to go to war with Iraq. That is not what Security Council Resolution 678 said."[77] Yet the resolution *had* said something very much like that. It authorized member states to use "all necessary means" to uphold previous resolutions calling for Iraq's withdrawal from Kuwait.[78]

Moynihan similarly criticized the North American Treaty Organization's 1999 humanitarian intervention in Kosovo, by which the alliance "attacked a sovereign state in what would seem a clear avoidance of the terms of the U.N. Charter." He continued, perhaps regretfully implying the need for a change in existing international law but nonetheless acknowledging its authority: "Even so, it remains the case that the present state of international law is in significant ways a limitation on our freedom to pursue humanitarian purposes. Again, a matter that calls for attention, indeed, demands attention." He concluded on a Burkean note that summarized a career-long commitment on the issue: "In sum, limits and law."[79]

These would also be the keys to addressing the most seemingly intractable problem of the new world order—ethnicity.

"POOR LITTLE DEVILS"

National self-determination, again, was one of the two ideals Wilson thrust on the twentieth century, international law being the other. But even though self-determination enjoyed immense success—as Moynihan wrote, few nations dared speak of themselves except in Wilsonian terms[80]—it was also immensely problematic. "America let loose this idea upon the world and it is now pretty much what the world thinks. It has to be insisted, however, that this is a surpassingly fuzzy idea. There is no satisfactory answer to the question as to what self-determination, as more or less guaranteed by the U.N. Charter, actually *means*."[81] There were, for example, 171 nations in the world but 6,170 languages. It seemed unreasonable to believe self-determination meant there would someday be 6,170 nations, but more than 171 seemed likely. The question was how many and by what standard—and the high-minded ideals of Wilson provided scant guidance.[82]

Yet Wilsonianism *had* created expectations that were straining to be met. The standard narrative was that Marxism had long suppressed them in the name of class conflict. Moynihan disagreed. Glazer had established that communism in the United States was essentially an ethnic phenomenon. "What Karl Marx wrote in the British Museum, Nathan Glazer disproved in the New York Public Library," Moynihan remarked with trademark wit, "but while you see, or used to see, statues of Marx all over the place, you hardly ever see a statue of Nathan Glazer."[83] Moynihan saw essentially the same phenomenon operating in international politics: "I would offer the proposition that in the often incredibly heterogeneous former colonies that obtained independence following the Second World War, Marxism provided a rationale for rule by the dominant ethnic group." It was, after all, a doctrine uniquely suited to domination.[84]

With the collapse of Marxism, then, came the collapse of that rationale and therefore the unleashing of ethnic conflict. Moynihan's primary purpose apparently was to identify the phenomenon, solutions to it being elusive and his Burkean disposition perhaps inhibiting any search for a panacea. Indeed, his appreciation of ethnicity was itself a deeply Burkean commitment rooted in a deferral to circumstance. But international law and organization could at least provide an objective means for adjudicating and perhaps even policing ethnic disputes.[85] Indeed, international law might have been a predicate for the survival of ethnically rooted states such as Israel, for it grounded their legitimacy.[86]

Still, prudence was in order. Self-determination, as Wilson's secretary of state Robert Lansing had written, was "loaded with dynamite." The United States would have to restrain its own hopes, Moynihan wrote:

It will also be necessary for the United States and also, even, the democracies of Western Europe to reconsider what Reinhold

Niebuhr once called "The Myth of Democratic Universality," the idea that democracy is a "universal option for all nations." Civil rights preceded political rights in the West, and this may be the most that can be hoped for in many of the new states. . . . Stratified systems of governance, call it federalism where appropriate, are clearly a necessity if any order is to emerge from the proximate confusion.[87]

Here, Moynihan may have been more scholar than statesman, seeking, as he had on the issue of poverty in the late 1960s, to shift modes of thought rather than offer precise solutions. The exact contours of "stratified systems of governments" were unclear. This was apparently Moynihan's attempt to blend self-governance with multiethnic states. Just as he had written with ethnicity at home, it did not need to be destructive—it might even be a force for good—in the international realm. "There is nothing wrong—everything right—with an intelligent, responsible self-respect, even self-regard," he declared. "The challenge is to make the world safe for and from ethnicity, safe for just those differences which large assemblies, democratic or otherwise, will typically attempt to suppress."[88]

The international community would still have to be prepared to steel itself against atrocity. But it also had to accept that difficult times were ahead. He concluded his book on the subject, *Pandaemonium*, by noting, "For the moment the more pressing matter is simply to contain the risk, to restrain the tendency to hope for too much, either of altruism or of common sense. Pandaemonium was inhabited by creatures quite convinced that the great Satan had their best interests at heart. Poor little devils."[89]

SECRECY AND SECURITY

Moynihan remarked several times that the ethnic perspective had made it possible to forecast the breakup of the Soviet Union. But another question nagged at him: why had the vaunted intelligence services of the

United States so utterly failed to do so? The answer he found was that they were so enveloped in secrecy that they were insulated from outside perspectives, such as the warnings he had been sounding on the topic since 1979—and, indeed, such as the commonsense observation, evident to "any taxi driver in Berlin," that the East German economy could not possibly be larger than its West German counterpart, a claim the CIA held as dogma nearly until the fall of the Berlin Wall.[90] Moynihan had tried: in speeches, in floor statements, even as an observer to the Strategic Arms Reduction Talks in Geneva, asking American negotiators what made them think there would be a Soviet Union ("no reply").[91] "Official Washington simply could not *hear* what I was saying," he recalled. "No one said I was wrong, it is simply that no one could pick up a signal on that frequency."[92]

In his book *Secrecy: The American Experience,* arising from his chairmanship of the Commission on Protecting and Reducing Government Secrecy, Moynihan reformulated the problem: "Secrecy is a form of regulation." In domestic affairs, "government prescribes what the citizen may do." In foreign affairs, "government prescribes what the citizen may know."[93] Bureaucracies treated secrecy in Weberian terms, as assets to be hoarded and traded. He used, as an example, the hoarding of the Venona intercepts—intelligence that enabled the FBI to identify communist infiltration, including Alger Hiss's guilt, as early as the Truman administration. This was information that, if revealed, might have spared the nation a half century–long culture war over the case.[94]

Moreover, Moynihan said, the quality of American intelligence had seemingly declined despite massive investments in it. The intelligence community had consistently overstated the communist threat and completely missed the Soviet collapse. As early as the 1960s, with the communist powers "well advanced in venomous assessments of treachery by one another," the intelligence community "saw instead a human wave of ecstatic red soldiery waving ancient rifles on their united way South."[95]

How did the CIA so consistently misstate the dangers? "The answer has to be, at least in part," he asserted, "that too much of the information was secret, not sufficiently open to critique by persons outside government."[96] Yet the executive branch of government inherently resisted reform, not merely because of bureaucratic entrenchment but also because presidents themselves became proprietary defenders of the CIA. "No president is going to get rid of the CIA," Moynihan said. "A daily diet of SECRETS that no one knows but him and his closest associates."[97] As a result, a Cold War intelligence bureaucracy had survived the end of the Cold War. (Moynihan introduced two bills to abolish the CIA and reassign its analysis functions to the State Department. He was treated as an eccentric.)[98]

Moynihan's commission proposed a two-part framework for governing the use of secrecy. First, information should be classified "only if its protection is demonstrably in the interests of national security, with the goal of keeping classification to an absolute minimum." Second, "a declassification system should be established" under which information would not be classified for longer than ten years unless it was specifically reclassified due to current risks. No information would remain classified after thirty years unless it could be shown that declassification would "harm an individual or ongoing government activities."[99] Moynihan granted that secrecy remained necessary. The problem was a "culture of secrecy" that treated classification as a norm. He remarked, "The central fact is that we live today in an Information Age. Open sources give us the vast majority of what we need to know in order to make intelligent decisions." Burke would have recognized Moynihan's characterization of these choices as "decisions made by people at ease with disagreement and ambiguity and tentativeness."[100]

Moynihan almost certainly would be dismayed at the resurgence of secrecy surrounding the topic to which, with unavoidable speculation—for he only briefly witnessed it—we now turn.

THE AGE OF TERRORISM

Moynihan had written on the topic of terrorism before 9/11. Terrorism, he argued in 1985, was a crime to be dealt with under international law, another reason for the United States not to abrogate that device.[101] In the 1990s, he recognized the anti-Western hostility of Islamic radicals as a manifestation of ethnic conflict in the post-Soviet era.[102] In a post-9/11 op-ed for the *Washington Post,* suggestively entitled ETHNICITY NOW, Moynihan's tone was sober, but he emphasized perspective and calm: "The world out there is now in here, and nothing will ever be the same. The test now will be for us to get straight just what it is 'out there.' The answer is ethnicity, but this has proved hard to learn." Islam, he wrote, ought not be "baffling." Nearly every Islamic state was under European rule at the beginning of the twentieth century, and "now is the time of revenge; nothing will change this." Yet there was good news, too. The terrorists also terrified many Islamic states; these potential allies should be cultivated. "And keep in mind: We are a singularly successful multi-ethnic society," he added. "We have a vibrant Islamic community of emigrants from across the world. They will be heard in those parts of the world they come from, and they can speak out." He concluded by invoking the words of an old friend: "But most important of all is to follow the counsel of Donald Rumsfeld . . . : 'Do not allow terrorism to alter our own way of life.'"[103]

However, Moynihan would soon be discouraged on this front, just as he had been in the past. He felt Congress overreacted to the Oklahoma City bombing of 1995 by limiting habeas corpus petitions in terrorism-related death penalty cases. In Senate debate, he called the writ of habeas corpus "one of the fundamental civil liberties on which every democratic society of the world has built political liberties that have come subsequently."[104] On the international terrorism front, he advised in 1995 "that we keep cool heads": "*Steady On.* Do not panic and do precisely what the terrorists—and our totalitarian adversaries—want to provoke us to do, which is to become more like them. Both terrorists and totalitarians are guided by similar principles; they are equally contemptible of democracy and individual liberty. They succeed only to the extent that we abandon our principles and become more violent or less free."[105]

He seemed nearly to foresee what was coming: "We have to understand that, as the most powerful and prosperous country in the world, the United States and Americans are going to be the object of terrorist attacks for the foreseeable future. . . . But let's not interrupt the most important activities of our society every time some of these lunatics commit an atrocity."[106] In 2000, he rued intrusive security measures that separated Americans from the US Capitol: "Somehow we have got to recover our nerve; shaken really since November 22, 1963."[107]

Deducing how Moynihan would have viewed subsequent debates in antiterrorism policy—on military detention, torture, and so forth—is an inherently speculative and therefore chancy affair. His devotion to the writ of habeas corpus is suggestive. So is his pre-9/11 insistence on keeping cool heads, something he also suggested at least in tenor in the immediate aftermath of the attack. Moynihan almost certainly would have objected to the post-9/11 proliferation of secrecy. What is wholly clear, for he actually said it, is that he believed society was circumscribing freedom in ways that rewarded terrorism and inhibited citizenship.

In 2003, one month before his death, he was invited to speak on his Guiding Principles for Federal Architecture at the Ronald Reagan Building and International Trade Center. He recalled the tightening of liberties during the Cold War. "A real enough threat," he said of the Soviets. "But our response was not always realistic. Now we confront terrorism. Worldwide, sinister, secretive. Much as was the earlier threat. And also internal. We must not lose our nerve, as we did more than once in the course of that earlier trial." He reviewed the security procedures at the Reagan Building: magnetometers, pat-downs, X-rays. Moreover, he said, "Congress has called for a 'national watch list center,' whatever that is." Libraries, office buildings, even the lighting of the national Christmas tree were encircled in security. Part of the problem, he suggested, was the unwillingness of society to accept the risk that naturally attended openness:

> Can we not grasp this? Do we want to teach our children you must be checked by an armed guard in order to read a book? Or gaze in wonder at a giant Christmas tree?

There are indeed buildings that need to be secured. And not a few.

But there are places in the public square that do not need that. Might something go wrong? Yes. Nothing new. But the stability of the American National Government is not served by an intimidated citizenry.

"Add that," he emphatically concluded, by way of bringing one of his final public reflections around to one of his first and most enduring public contributions, "to the Principles."[108]

4. Toward a Burkean Liberalism

The thought that we have genuine control over events is as much a
delusion as the conviction that we are helpless in the face of the inevitable.

—Moynihan, *Saturday Evening Post*, 1968

On February 4, 1994, the Senate took up the seemingly benign Educate
America Act, by which the Congress declared a series of goals American
schoolchildren would attain by the year 2000. The bill passed overwhelmingly. Moynihan, who indicated he would not object in vain,
nonetheless briefly spoiled the self-congratulation that preceded it. Addressing the presiding officer and reading the quantifiable items among
the goals itemized in the act, he declared in sequence, "Madam President,
that will not happen."[1] The goals had all the credibility of Soviet grain es-
timates. He knew. He had studied the Coleman Report on Equality of
Educational Opportunity at length in a Harvard seminar—had run the
numbers, scrutinized the data, confirmed the findings—and he understood that infusions of resources and declarations of demands, though
gratifying to Congress, were not the point. Family was.

This was not new. Moynihan had written a reflection on education
policy for the *Public Interest* in 1991 in which he identified an overly sim-
plistic "deficiency model" of the War on Poverty: "Poverty persisted because certain young people received too little education. The solution:
give them more."[2] The Coleman Report had not been available at the
time, he noted, but it probably would not have mattered, for interest
groups were clamoring for resources. Grandiose proclamations of goals
were "mindless" forms of "avoidance." President George H. W. Bush had
already declared goals for 2000; these, in turn, "would have been more
defensible were it not for the fact that in 1984 the preceding president
had set out substantially the same goals for 1990."

Here, we might expect to encounter a cynic in Moynihan. If so, we would not be encountering a Burkean. Burke was a reformer—a conserving reformer, to be sure, but a reformer nonetheless. Moynihan retained his robust confidence in the capacity of government to facilitate improvements, albeit gradual ones, in even the most seemingly intractable problems. He rejected, as expressed in the epigraph to this chapter, both utopianism *and* defeatism. Government could play a productive role in addressing problems only if it remained open to evidence on the complexity of their nature.

As a metaphor, his treatment of the education goals is suggestive on a number of fronts. It illustrates Moynihan's rejection of perfectionist proclamations in the face of intricate social systems. It is a reminder of the primacy of subsidiary institutions such as family in his thought and of the particular blend of Burkeanism and liberalism evident in his esteem for those institutions, even as he maintained his faith in the capacity of government to nourish them. And it shows his belief that policy needed to be grounded not in abstraction, such as the year 2000 goals, but in concrete experience.

Therein lie the elements of a Burkean liberalism inspired by Moynihan but not, in its specifics, herein attributed to him—and, more generally, a Burkean revival, the terms of a constructive conversation between Burkeans of different views based on respect for systems, subsidiarity, and circumstance.

SYSTEMS

"Cities," Moynihan wrote, "are complex social systems. Interventions that, intentionally or not, affect one component of the system almost invariably affect the second, third, and fourth components as well, and these in turn affect the first component, often in ways quite opposite the direction of the initial intervention."[3] The observation was Burkean to its core. Burke wrote: "The real effects of moral causes are not always immediate; but that which in the first instance is prejudicial may be excellent in its remoter operation. . . . The reverse also happens; and very plausible schemes, with very pleasing commencements, have often shameful and lamentable conclusions."[4]

For both Moynihan and Burke, the complexity of these social systems arose from their gradual and organic evolution over time as opposed to their rational and conscious construction. Burke was unable to see in "the scheme of a republic . . . the work of a [single] comprehensive and disposing mind, or even the provisions of a vulgar prudence."[5] With his friend Michael Polanyi, Moynihan rejected the radical view that, in the words of the former approvingly quoted by the latter, "if society is not a divine institution, it is made by man, and man is free to do with society what he likes. There is then no excuse for having a bad society, and we must make a good one without delay." This was, for both Polanyi and Moynihan, simple cover for seizing power and for regarding any resistance to that move as, again in the former's words, "high treason." Moynihan attributed this spirit to the triumph of Enlightenment rationalism over religion. For assessing the extent of his Burkean disposition, it is significant that he endorsed Polanyi's attribution of this process to Burke's intellectual antipode Jean-Jacques Rousseau, who, on Polanyi's analysis, invested rationalism with the "supreme hopes of Christianity," untethered from the grounding weight of "their dogmatic framework."[6]

Moynihan also warned that Enlightenment rationalism alone might not be capable of sustaining liberalism, for the belief in individual dignity at liberalism's core depended on transcendent values:

In a demystified world, science remains the only authority; and the authority of science, which liberalism did so much to promote, does not now speak unambiguously in its favor. We regard the enlightened deism of Jefferson with perhaps more tolerance, but with the same skepticism, as that with which he viewed the fervent faith of the Middle Ages. While the religious beliefs which underlay our political order, in particular the belief in the infinite value of each soul as a moral agent, still retain strength among some, they do not have the power to convince others.[7]

A Burkean liberalism must blend Moynihan's simultaneous confidence in the capacity of the public sector to improve society with his respect for the complexity of social systems and the consequent need, at least generally, to reform them incrementally. This is fundamentally a posture of humility. James Q. Wilson put Moynihan's outlook in the following way, also in terms hospitable to Burke: "Perhaps man in the future will be smarter than man in the past. But until somebody can show us that the new man will be smarter than the old one, it is very hard for a thoughtful person to embrace untested changes. And Pat is a thoughtful person."[8] Burke, similarly, would speak of the "tender parental solicitude which fears to cut up the infant for the sake of an experiment."[9] This is not to say Burke or Moynihan resisted improvement or that Burkean liberalism would. What they resisted was sudden, jolting, dramatic change. Burke wrote of "preserving the method of nature in the conduct of the state"—gradual evolution that built upon the past, conserving as it reformed—such that "in what we improve we are never wholly new; in what we retain, we are never wholly obsolete."[10]

Because of its emphasis on gradualism, Burkean liberalism also resists the rhetoric of catastrophe. Moynihan wrote: "When situations of considerable but not impossible difficulty are described in apocalyptic terms, responses tend to be erratic, even convulsive, and even if, by fortune or design, the difficulties lessen, there is no vocabulary at hand by which to describe such incremental change."[11] For the same reason, the Burkean liberal would acknowledge progress where it occurred. Acknowledging increments of progress was a necessary precondition for future progress; by contrast, the motive for refusing to do so, Moynihan said, was usually the accumulation of power:

> What then are the "problems poorly stated" of our time? They are various but have, it seems to me, a unifying characteristic; namely, the rejection by those seeking a more just, more equal society of any indications that our society is in fact becoming more just and more equal. Society is seen in ahistorical terms: what is not altogether acceptable is altogether unacceptable; gradations are ignored and

incremental movements are scorned. Those who by disposition are incrementalists, or for whom the contemplation of society has led to a conviction that incremental change is a necessity, not a choice, in human affairs, are baffled by this attitude and resentful of it.[12]

Burkean liberalism will for related reasons resist efforts to shove public discourse to Manichaean absolutes that politics rarely, especially in its workaday mode, occupies with any clarity. "All government, indeed every human benefit and enjoyment, every virtue, and every prudent act," Burke declared in his "Speech on Conciliation with the Colonies," "is founded on compromise and barter. We balance inconveniences; we give and take; we remit some rights, that we may enjoy others; and we choose rather to be happy citizens, than subtle disputants."[13] Moralized politics accommodates neither diffusion of power nor its concomitant compromise, "which," Burke wrote, "naturally begets moderation."[14]

Because social systems were complex, Moynihan counseled that the craft of politics pertained not to wholesale social transformation but rather to looking just a little bit ahead into the future. ("In a chess master [looking ahead] involves considerable intellectual elegance, but politics is mostly checkers.")[15] Yet politics, and not just liberal politics, was increasingly hostile both to that kind of humility and to that other, related key to the Burkeanism of Moynihan's politics: limitation. Moynihan's reformulation of Kennedy's inaugural address—"Suppose [Kennedy] had said, 'Things are complicated over here . . . '"—would not rouse voters from their television sets to the ballot boxes. Nor would Moynihan's dictum that politicians' "achievement can never be more than relatively good"[16] (like Burke's dictum that "nothing universal can be rationally affirmed on any moral or any political subject").[17]

Instead, we demand grandiosity from political figures, and it is a myth that liberals alone indulge it. The proper response to a liberal utopian scheme has become a conservative utopian scheme. The phrase "perhaps government can't do that, or can't do it on an electoral time line or within constitutional constraints" has been expunged from our political vocabulary. One reason is surely that incremental change requires patience. "Even the most rapid social change, as seen from the perspective of history," Moynihan wrote, "comes slowly, one step at a time, from the point of view of the individual demanding it."[18]

Appreciation of complexity also requires a prudent awareness of the possibility of unintended consequences, a certain dispositional conservatism—deliberately rendered here in the lowercase—with respect to both ambition and expectations for social reform. There is no reason, as Moynihan showed, this insight cannot be equally available to liberals and conservatives. They can disagree on the generosity of the state while still concurring that it ought to move tentatively and to be wary of disrupting long-standing, especially slowly evolved and complex, arrangements and institutions. This complexity of society requires, in turn, a certain simplicity of political plans. "Political ideas," Moynihan wrote, "must be simple. Which is not to say they must be facile. To the contrary, the most profound propositions are often the simplest as well."[19] Attempts to micromanage the terms of social reform—which liberals have generally undertaken through outright prescription but which conservatives have been as willing to incentivize by complicating the tax code—are inevitably disruptive in ways that cannot be anticipated.

It should be emphasized that the relevant Burkean issue is not the generosity of government—though, clearly, that too imposes consequences foreseen and unforeseen and is a proper topic on philosophical grounds of liberal-conservative debate—but rather its complexity. Moynihan, paraphrasing Glazer, observed a tension between "increasing insistence on individual freedom and demands for ever more complex forms of social intervention."[20] That he opposed freedom to complexity rather than to generosity is significant. Social Security, of which Moynihan was an ardent defender, is generous but simple. Its fiscal problems are well known, but precisely because of its simplicity, they are also, as Moynihan emphasized, not difficult—only controversial—to address. Their consequences, too, though also controversial, are not difficult to predict.

A Burkean liberalism, then, recognizes that the application of convoluted solutions to infinitely complex systems from a desire to dictate the

precise terms of social reform invites, if not assures, unintended consequences. The services strategy of the War on Poverty comes to mind in
this context, and one wonders as a result whether Moynihan did not
give up too easily on the guaranteed income. Subsequent analyses of the
SIME-DIME data have questioned the conclusion that it stimulated
family dissolution—the conclusion that triggered Moynihan's disavowal
of the proposal.[21] Other commentators have argued that the families in
question were unstable to begin with and that, if anything, the addition
of income merely accelerated, rather than instigated, the inevitable. To
the extent the data do show a tendency toward family breakup—and
this is overwhelmingly the direction in which analyses lean—perhaps a
guaranteed income might be modified to contain incentives for family
cohesion. On the whole, given the sad tendency toward family dissolution regardless of policy, the political and constitutional benefits of simplicity may outweigh its costs.

Perhaps for that reason, the guaranteed income has enjoyed a revival in some conservative circles—those on which Moynihan, following Milton Friedman's negative income tax, originally drew—as a
simple, transparent, and noncoercive alternative to a control-oriented
welfare system laden with bureaucracy, compulsion, or public intru-
sion into subsidiary institutions. The idea exhibits certain Burkean
characteristics, including a respect for social complexity and the renun-
ciation of attempts to manipulate it, such that the difference between a
conservative and a liberal manifestation of it may pertain simply to its
generosity.

To be sure, the idea cannot be imputed to Burke, who, though devoted to the poor and oppressed (as those in Ireland and India), preferred private charity to public relief.[22] Moynihan, separated by nearly
two centuries of political and economic circumstance, believed—and
no conservative in the mainstream of contemporary electoral politics
disagrees with him; the dispute is about particulars—that private charity simply could not cope with the scale of dislocation entailed in modern markets. Still, within a contemporary context, there is a Burkean
flavor to the guaranteed income. Despite some of Moynihan's early

rhetoric surrounding it, the concept is not utopian and is perhaps even antiutopian, which is to say, in Lowi's terms, it aims merely to alleviate rather than to eliminate poverty. It accepts social complexity rather than attempting to modify it. It is not free of the possibility of unintended consequences—the SIME-DIME experiment showed that—but its relative simplicity at least enables their evaluation.

Because social systems are complex, Burkean liberalism also approaches the welfare state with a degree of deference and caution. The Burkean liberal will recognize its flaws, including its fiscal fragility—one of Moynihan's last public assignments was to serve on President George W. Bush's Commission to Strengthen Social Security—and any demonstrable social ills that emanate from it, as empirical limitations on social policy. But he or she will also approach its reform with both respect for its achievements and caution about its complexity. The New Deal regime has now been an integral part of American society for more than seventy-five years. Its offspring, the Great Society, has, however flawed, extended its reach into American institutions for fifty—more than a fifth of US constitutional history. It is here. Expectations have formed around it. Of course, the Burkean is not obligated to acquiesce simply because it exists, but he or she will approach its modification with a degree of caution and regard. Moynihan thus argued that genuine conservatives opposed the 1996 welfare reform because of its suddenness and unforeseeable consequences: "The principal—and most principled—opponents of this legislation [have been] conservative social scientists who for years have argued against liberal nostrums for changing society with the argument that no one knows enough to mechanistically change society."[23]

Moynihan described the relevant "sensibility [as] not so much a great *caution,* as great *care.*"[24] Note that this sensibility is compatible with liberalism; perhaps the distinction between Burkean liberalism and conservatism is one of degree. In either case, this sensibility does challenge traditional Progressivism in one central way: its temporal orientation is rooted not just in transformation, of which Burkean liberalism is skeptical, but also in tradition, from which it believes it can learn. In other words, the Burkean liberal, though looking forward—just a little bit, as Moynihan wrote—also looks back. This requires a reorientation of reason from a priori logic toward what Burke called the "collected reason of ages," by which he meant not blind deference to tradition but rather respect for the multivariate application of principle to unfolding circumstance.[25] By contrast, Oakeshott's Rationalist, of whom Moynihan was suspicious, feels, Oakeshott wrote, "a deep distrust of time, an impatient hunger for eternity and an irritable nervousness in the face of everything topical and transitory." He resists tradition and experience in favor of the sanctity of his own reason, despite the obvious entwinement of politics with "the traditional, the circumstantial and the transitory."[26]

Burke instead offered the dictum that society was a contract between "those who are dead, those who are living, and those who are to be born."[27] He warned that by operating on a model of rapid and unprincipled change, "the whole chain and continuity of the commonwealth would be broken. No one generation could link with the other. Men would become little better than the flies of a summer."[28] Moynihan, reacting with contempt to the failed utopianism of the community action programs in the War on Poverty, found similar authority in the links between generations: "For those who practice the most demanding calling of all, that of government itself . . . Edmund Burke's conception of successive generations possessing their society's laws and customs of governance in the form of an entailed estate, given them for lifetime use, with the condition that it be passed on at least not diminished and hopefully enhanced, seems especially relevant now in the United States."[29]

This metaphor of inheritance, according to Burke, "furnishes a sure principle of conservation, and a sure principle of transmission; without at all excluding a principle of improvement."[30] Burkean liberalism and conservatism are separated by the extent of their confidence in government to facilitate that improvement. Moynihan's confidence was, it might be said, pragmatic but persistent. He recognized the limits of government but never lost his devotion to it as an agent of common endeavor and shared responsibility. This latter point—responsibility—is a vital one. Moynihan believed that people were responsible for one another and that government could—and ought to—aid in executing that obligation. There was dignity in it doing so.

Burkean liberalism is distinguished from Progressivism not merely by its temporal orientation but also by the extent of its faith in reason. Moynihan might be easily mistaken as prone to the Progressive quest for scientific or technical solutions to political problems. He was not. His confidence in social science was, as we have seen, retrospective and evaluative rather than prospective and prescriptive. It was thus inextricably bound up with experience and the gradualism that a Burkean reliance on experience implies.

Rationalist politics, on Oakeshott's account, was given to two qualities that are also incompatible with Burkean liberalism. One was perfectionism. The Rationalist, Oakeshott wrote in an essay with which Moynihan was familiar, "is not devoid of humility; he can imagine a problem which would remain impervious to the onslaught of his own reason. But what he cannot imagine is politics which do not consist in solving problems, or a political problem of which there is no 'rational' solution at all." The Progressive will seek transformative panaceas in such situations, whereas the Burkean liberal will opt for amelioration of the symptoms rather than a cure for the disease: the income strategy, for instance, not the services strategy. The second characteristic of rationalism, which Oakeshott took to be entwined with perfectionism and which the Burkean liberal, such as Moynihan, must also discard, was uniformity. "A scheme which does not recognize circumstance can have no place for variety," Oakeshott asserted.[31] Variety, we recall, was among the values Moynihan imputed to the principle of subsidiarity—the next pillar of Burkean liberalism.

SUBSIDIARITY

Subsidiarity reflects the clearest and most persistent influence of Catholic thought on Moynihan's politics. It has sometimes been taken to be a counsel of laissez-faire: in order that subsidiary institutions may be strengthened, larger and more distant institutions such as government should retreat. Moynihan's contention—the space a Burkean liberalism may occupy—was that government could nourish these institutions and enable them better to play their vital roles. Robert Nisbet argued similarly in *The Quest for Community* that the role of modern democracies would be to "reinforce these [subsidiary] associations, to provide, administratively, a means whereby the normal competition of group differences is held within bounds and an environment of law within which no single authority, religious or economic, shall attain a repressive and monopolistic influence."[32] Moynihan saw the family at the center of these buffering forces but also sought a public role in reinforcing the full array of institutions that radiated outward from it, what his friend James Coleman called the "microstructures of society." Moynihan explained: "Families are only one institution among many. They are a part of a neighborhood, one element in several types of communities—schools, churches, cultural and political. If those communities are weak, the family cannot be strong."[33]

Burkean liberalism, then, recognizes both that subsidiarity is key to social health *and* that government can help sustain subsidiary institutions. Moynihan did not mean subsidizing these institutions, nor does Burkean liberalism—nothing so simple or potentially corrosive as that. Rather, the point is more that a purely hands-off policy in the name of subsidiarity is not necessarily as neutral as it claims to be. Just as government cannot help but have policies that affect families, it cannot help but have policies that affect subsidiary institutions. Nonprofit organizations, for example, "are powerfully affected, sometimes for good, but sometimes for ill, by laws and regulations of the Federal Government." "The charitable impulse is a precious thing, and it is essentially a private impulse," Moynihan observed, "[but] it, too, can be powerfully affected by public policy"[34]—and government ought to choose these policies consciously and carefully.

Burkean liberalism welcomes a constructive role for government where it can play one, but it resists statist solutions—that is, those that are conducive to Tocqueville's reduction of democratic society to a bipolar relation of the individual to the state, with no mediating institutions in between. Speaking to the AFL-CIO as UN ambassador, Moynihan denounced totalitarianism in Tocquevillian terms, describing it as hostile not just to individual liberty but also to subsidiary institutions. This was a premonition of statism:

> What is going on is a systematic effort to create an international society in which government is the one and only legitimate institution. The old dream of an international economic order in which one single nation dominated is being replaced by a not different vision of the domination of a single idea, the idea of the all-encompassing state, a state which has no provision for the liberties of individuals, much less for the liberties of collections of individuals, such as trade unions.[35]

These "collections of individuals" whose liberty Moynihan wanted to defend formed the heart of subsidiarity. The policy choices he preferred, such as an "above the line" deduction that enabled those who did not itemize to deduct charitable donations from their taxes, would have nourished these collections and resisted statism. Similarly, a guaranteed income as Moynihan conceived it was liberal without being statist, insofar as it involved the state in a common provision while also, crucially, remaining neutral as to its precise uses and discouraging dependence by rewarding work. Its intent was empowerment and variety, rather than coercion and uniformity. The services strategy, by contrast, was statist in that it left the individual not only wholly dependent but, in Tocquevillian terms, wholly enervated, and consequently, his or her capacity for freedom and initiative atrophied from disuse.

Burkean liberalism must also adopt at least a questioning posture toward statism associated with security because that goal has been historically associated with the inflation of the state and the subsumption of the individual and because it is given to the moralistic politics Burke and Moynihan likewise resisted as conducive to radical absolutes.

Moynihan briefly commented on the post-9/11 security regime, but he saw its tendencies long before in the pretensions of the Secret Service, the proliferation of secrecy, and the tendency toward militarization evident in periods ranging from World War I to the Cold War.

A Burkean liberalism rooted in subsidiarity also values the vitality of private systems of authority as Nisbet conceived of the term—not as raw power, which is precisely what Nisbet did not mean, but rather as voluntary relationships grounded in tradition. Moynihan stated, "It is in the nature of authority, as Robert A. Nisbet continues to remind us, that it is consensual, that it is not coercive. When authority systems collapse they are replaced by power systems, which are coercive."[36] As Catholic social thought emphasized, the individual becomes ultimately attached to the wider society by means of these subsidiary relationships. The passage in Burke to which Moynihan most liked to allude describes the process: "To be attached to the subdivision, to love the little platoon we belong to in society, is the first principle (the germ as it were) of public affections. It is the first link in the series by which we proceed towards a love to our country and to mankind."[37]

As Tocqueville teaches, an immense difference obtains between the individual becoming linked to the society as a whole directly rather than via buffering institutions. Subsidiary institutions add the elements of humanity and responsibility. They stimulate individual initiative and preserve difference. Direct attachment to the society, by contrast, is a faceless and vacuous relationship given to dependence, vulnerability, and power. It is for precisely this reason that Tocqueville—whose *Democracy in America* was, Moynihan wrote, "an unfailing source of insight and wisdom"[38]—was so taken with the American system of federalism and that the Burkean liberal must be devoted to its preservation.

This is not to say Burkean liberalism will simply reflexively seek to push all decisions downward, something Moynihan resisted as a poorly veiled attempt to emasculate programs, especially in the area of welfare. Instead, it is to say that the Burkean liberal should prefer, ceteris paribus, that policies be competently executed locally whenever possible. This is not, as Moynihan emphasized, a principle of competence or efficiency. The relevant principle is moral: decisions should be made as close as possible to the individual in order to preserve the initiative, identity, and dignity of individuals and the institutions that surround them—all values Moynihan associated with liberalism.

Subsidiary attachments also help to mitigate another problem arising from complexity—unanticipated consequences. As Moynihan put it, "Large-scale public interventions, large-scale economic developments disrupt things even as they are seen to improve them, and that disruption requires attention from what Edmund Burke called 'the small platoons' of a nation."[39] Society on the macro scale, that is, is largely unpredictable, but Coleman's micro structures are reliable. This reliance on families to mitigate social ills—to buffer the individual against the battering of social forces—is, in turn, a form of amelioration rather than wholesale transformation.

Yet Burkean liberalism also will combine federalism—and its attendant values of pluralism, variety, and experimentation—with underlying national commitments, again as a matter of moral principle, not just policy. Moynihan suggested the public commitment had to be made where benefits were due as a matter of "right," a concept he at varying times construed expansively—as, for example, by extending it to employment.[40] Such was the case for dependent children. The issue there, recall, was not whether the states would be allowed to vary their welfare policies, an authority Moynihan himself had written into law eight years prior to the 1996 reform. It was whether the national government would preserve aid to dependent children as an entitlement whose funding was guaranteed to rise with their need.

It should be observed that for Moynihan, subsidiarity was not a matter of simple *opposition* between the public and private spheres. Public and private institutions did not need to detract from each other; they might actually reinforce one another. Significantly, Moynihan associated this view with Burke, asking: "Is it not possible that, by nourishing the private, non-profit sector, we may in the end also increase the vigor of the public sector? Is it indeed true that the only way to more effective, responsive government and to a more just and humane society lies in further constricting and denying the private sector? Burke would not have thought so. Nor do I."[41]

Subsidiarity also demands a rejection of the modern ethos of radical individualism, an area in which contemporary conservatism's emphasis on abstract economic rights has broken with its Burkean roots. Moynihan was clearly devoted to the dignity of the individual, a principle he defended against totalitarianism: "Ours is a culture based on the primacy of the individual—the rights of the individual, the welfare of the individual, the claims of the individual against those of the state."[42] But it was, again, the person attached to the society through subsidiary institutions, not the atomized individual merely floating free. "From Durkheim," he noted, "we have the proposition that no purely contractual society can arise or continue to exist. ('A dust of individuals.')" Individual hedonism could not produce sufficient obligation to the wider society without "inputs from families."[43]

Subsidiarity offers another advantage. It roots politics in the concrete rather than the abstract. Hence the final condition of Burkean liberalism—respect for the limiting conditions of circumstance.

CIRCUMSTANCE

A politics bounded by circumstance, as opposed to one based on abstract principle, is inherently a politics of limitation. "Nothing is good," Burke had written, "but in proportion and with reference."[44] Moynihan, too, had emphasized proportionality. "*Fiat justitia et ruat coelum* [Let justice be done though the heavens fall] ought to be more an abstract than an applied principle of government," he wrote.[45] On another occasion, quoting the same axiom, he suggested it be rendered: "If justice is done with sufficient regularity and moderation, the heavens need not fall. They might even rejoice in the nation that has shown a capacity for redemption and self-renewal."[46]

Burke had similarly declined to consider anything "in all the nakedness and solitude of metaphysical abstraction. Circumstances . . . give in reality to every political principle its distinguishing colour, and discriminating effect."[47] This was explicitly opposed to abstract reason: "Matters of prudence are under the dominion of circumstance, and not of logical analogies. It is absurd to take it otherwise."[48] A politics of circumstance was consequently moored to the concrete and, crucially, informed by it. Prudence for Burke arose from the application of judgment to circumstance, seasoned by experience. For Moynihan, the craft of government pertained to moments "when the matter at issue is less what *should* happen than what *will*. Persons in perfect accord on values may differ profoundly as between those of little experience and those of much. . . . On balance experience is instructive and directs one's thoughts as much to what may go wrong as to what may go right."[49]

That does not mean, of course, that Moynihan would have rendered all politics technocratic, still less that he would have regarded the choice of ends as superfluous. It is to say that the Aristotelian capacity to choose a path to a given end is indelibly shaped by experience. It is also to say that the mere "articulation of moral purpose," as Moynihan put it, may be necessary but is also insufficient for the complete exercise of political authority. Untethered to experience, moralizing may be especially prone to abuse. "There is, surely, a disposition among 'liberals' to be concerned with values, and a corresponding tendency among 'conservatives' to think about consequences," Moynihan said.[50] Politics required both. And Burkean liberalism lies at the intersection between them.

Put another way, of course, Burkeanism itself lies at that intersection, for the real issue is that the Burkean anywhere on the political spectrum is concerned with values rooted in circumstance. The values may differ, but circumstance, to which all sides in a political dispute have access, roots them in the concrete, experienced, and real. The radicalism that so repulsed Moynihan in the 1960s, a cousin—distant but still a genetic relation—to the Jacobinism of the French Revolution, surely arose in part from the fanciful flitting about of ideals unmoored from circumstance and consequence. The radical's devotion to abstractions such as equality licenses if not requires the sacrifice of seemingly subordinate values like, for example, academic freedom—or the sacrifice of worse, as Moynihan, whose Cambridge home, occupied by his wife and children as he worked in the Nixon White House, was threatened by campus radicals in 1970, knew.[51]

Burkean liberalism, then, will be concerned with consequences as they emerge through the medium of experience. This is an essential part of prudence. Moynihan accused the Reagan administration of lacking this quality in its fiscal policies because, contra the "new science of politics" of the Founders, which was rooted in realism and experience—"not pretty, but something far more important: predictable"—forward-looking ideology triumphed. "Ideology corrupted," and by corrupted, Moynihan explicitly meant that the administration stubbornly clung to its beliefs when evidence contradicted them. "Rather than give up its beliefs, the administration sacrificed its integrity." He continued: "Every dictate of theory, experience and prudence argued against 'gambling with history.' And yet it was done."[52] We are less concerned with the particulars of his critique of Reagan, especially since Moynihan applied the same hardheaded analysis to liberal programs such as Head Start and welfare, than with the significant compilation of "theory, experience and prudence"—including values and consequences—into a single set of concerns. The Burkean liberal, like Moynihan, is concerned with all three.

In the course of tying him to circumstance, we must be careful not to separate Moynihan (or, for that matter, Burke) from principle. Circumstance includes the reality of enduring principles. "Mankind," Moynihan said, "counts heavily on the permanence of things, and is rewarded for doing so."[53] Moreover, especially to the extent circumstance is transient, to respect it is not necessarily to acquiesce to it. "I surely," he wrote, "do not argue for a quietistic government acquiescing in whatever the tide of fortune or increments of miscalculation bring about—and in our time they have brought about hideous things."[54] He encountered circumstance, as Burke did, against the backdrop of clear and often nonnegotiable principles. Prudence serves higher goals; it is not one in itself. Certainly, Moynihan held firm to absolutes, such as the rights of individuals against totalitarianism and the federal commitment to impoverished children, which was the very essence of the United States going into opposition at the United Nations and of his nearly solo resistance to welfare reform in 1996. So did Burke.

Indeed, knowing when to take an ultimate stand itself required prudence. An impulse to capitulate under the cover of compromise was, according to Burke, "a false reptile prudence, the result not of caution but of fear." His description of the British urge to compromise with the revolutionary French sounds very much like Moynihan's denunciation of attempts to accommodate to totalitarianism. Under the influence of this false prudence, Burke wrote, "an abject distrust of ourselves, an extravagant admiration of the enemy, present us with no hope but in a compromise with his pride, by a submission to his will. This short plan of policy is the only counsel which will obtain a hearing."[55]

Because it must both adhere to principles and defer to circumstances, Burkean liberalism threads a course between what Moynihan regarded as Oakeshott's conservatism "to the point of passivity," on the one hand, and, on the other, transformational utopianism emanating from either side of the political spectrum. The anchoring weight of circumstance does not permit the buoyant, free-floating visions of utopianism. A politics that accepts such complexities as family as limiting conditions on educational attainment and ancient ethnic rivalries as barriers to harmonious living can afford only modest expectations. Burkean liberalism therefore believes in shared enterprise but chooses amelioration over transformation and progress over panaceas. It expects incremental improvement precisely because it retains confidence in both the capacity and the responsibility of society as a shared enterprise to undertake improving schemes. Its skepticism of ungrounded, abstract reasoning is among the bases for its insistence on responsible experimentation and retrospective analysis.

Circumstance is the criterion that most compellingly, although surely not exclusively, reminds us that Burkean liberalism is, after all, Burkean. And so we return to the question: how, finally, should we understand Daniel Patrick Moynihan? And, for that matter, how should we understand Edmund Burke?

"IT GOES ITS WAY"

Moynihan has been called a liberal and a conservative by those on either side who are eager to claim him and by those on opposite poles who seek to stigmatize him. Yet Moynihan was no chameleon; his commitments ran deep. Still less was he a simple flatterer: he was a competent politician, to be sure, but no one with his breadth of public writings and utterances could possibly have been all things to all people and gotten away with it. So what explains both his appeal and, in some circles, his offense to either side? Surely part of the answer is stylistic or, better put, methodological, which is to say that Moynihan represents a kind of politics—open to accommodation and evidence over ideology yet also interested in enduring ideas—that has always been rare but has, since his death in 2003, all but vanished. We need a Moynihan in reserve, and we especially could use one in the Senate, the institution designed to serve as a moderating, braking force—the one that makes the others stop and think.

But Moynihan's appeal to both sides also lies, or so this study asserts, in a Burkean disposition that has the capacity to draw certain strains of the contemporary Right and Left together. A Burkean liberal and a Burkean conservative, that is, may have more in common with each other than the former has with Progressives or the latter with, say, Tea Party restorationists. Moynihan's Social Security plan, which combined the certainty of public benefits with the opportunity for private investment accounts, supplies an example of how such a fusion might be expressed. The claim, again, is that the modifier *Burkean* may be more important than the label that follows. The Burkean liberal and Burkean conservative can debate the extent of government generosity; by contrast, the Burkean liberal and the Progressive, on one side, or the Burkean conservative and the Tea Party activist, on the other, are separated by the far wider chasms of the inherent desirability of dramatic change, the capacity of human reason to comprehend it, and the ability of complex social systems to accommodate to it.

To be sure, Moynihan was a liberal through and through. He believed in government as an agent of social improvement to an extent with which conservatives will disagree. He wanted activities undertaken in the public sector that conservatives would doubtless prefer to keep private. Similarly, although Burke the reformer was largely the province of liberals for much of the late nineteenth and early twentieth centuries—Woodrow Wilson, hardly a Burkean in any deep sense, was nonetheless a devotee because he identified with the reformer while overlooking the traditionalist—Russell Kirk was correct in reviving the Anglo-Irish statesman as a conservative.

The thesis of this book, then, is neither that Moynihan was a conservative nor that Burke was a liberal but rather that their views can accommodate one another and that American politics would be richer were this shared ground seeded and cultivated. That does not take, Moynihan insisted, any special skill, only a disposition that in its faith in government sounds liberal and in its respect for circumstance seems Burkean:

> There is a certain amount of genius in the world, and it goes its way, usually where few can follow. But the practice of government involves quite ordinary people of ordinary powers. In most circumstances such powers are adequate to the tasks at hand, given—such is my contention—a simple openness to alternative definitions or problems and a willingness to concede the possibility of events taking a variety of courses.[56]

There is, indeed, a certain amount of genius. It goes its way. Moynihan—redefining problems, respecting circumstances, breaking stone—went his. Most assuredly, none has followed.

Notes

PREFACE AND ACKNOWLEDGMENTS

1. Godfrey Hodgson, *The Gentleman from New York: Daniel Patrick Moynihan, A Biography* (New York: Houghton Mifflin, 2000).

INTRODUCTION: "AND YOU STILL BREAK STONE"

1. Joseph A. Schumpeter, *Capitalism, Socialism and Democracy* (New York: HarperCollins, 2008).

2. Daniel Patrick Moynihan, remarks to the chief volunteer officers and the chief professional officers, United Way of America, July 23, 1979, Daniel P. Moynihan Papers, Library of Congress, Washington, DC (hereafter Moynihan Papers). Again, I regret that I have not kept box numbers for the archival materials, but nearly all of them can be found chronologically in either the press or speech files.

3. Daniel Patrick Moynihan, *Coping: On the Practice of Government* (New York: Random House, 1973), 345.

4. Daniel Patrick Moynihan, *Toward a National Urban Policy* (New York: Basic Books, 1970), 12. He wrote of the same quotation in *Coping*: "A useful caution, and a goad to the further development of nonintuitive solutions" (p. 24).

5. Daniel Patrick Moynihan, "How the Great Society 'Destroyed the American Family,'" *Public Interest*, no. 108 (Summer 1992): 61.

6. Nathan Glazer, *The Limits of Social Policy* (Cambridge, MA: Harvard University Press, 1988), jacket blurb to the 1988 hardcover edition. Glazer's analysis was arguably far more pessimistic than Moynihan suggested.

7. Moynihan made this latter point in an October 4, 1978, speech to the Coalition of National Voluntary Associations, Moynihan Papers.

8. Daniel Patrick Moynihan, *Came the Revolution: Argument in the Reagan Era* (New York: Harcourt Brace Jovanovich, 1988), 6.

9. See Daniel Bell, *The End of Ideology: On the Exhaustion of Political Ideas in the Fifties* (Cambridge, MA: Harvard University Press, 2000), and Daniel

Patrick Moynihan, "On the Exhaustion of Political Ideas," address to the New York Academy of Sciences, December 8, 1977, Moynihan Papers.

10. Daniel Patrick Moynihan, *Maximum Feasible Misunderstanding: Community Action in the War on Poverty* (New York: Free Press, 1969), 8.

11. Moynihan, *Coping*, 255–256.

12. Daniel Patrick Moynihan, commencement address, University of Arkansas, May 11, 1991, Moynihan Papers.

13. Generally speaking, my references to the Great Society refer to its iteration in the War on Poverty; Moynihan was not a critic of the Great Society generally. He vigorously approved of Medicare and Medicaid, for example. It was the micromanagerial approach to poverty to which he objected.

14. Quoted in Richard A. Cloward and Frances Fox Piven, "The Welfare Vaudevillian," *Nation*, September 22, 1979, 236–239. As the headline indicates, the authors cited the quotation disapprovingly.

15. Burke: "Moderation will be stigmatized as the virtue of cowards, and compromise as the prudence of traitors"; see Edmund Burke, *Selected Works of Edmund Burke*, vol. 2, *Reflections on the Revolution in France* (Indianapolis, IN: Liberty Fund, 1999), 362.

16 Moynihan, *Coping*, 4 (limits as the basis of constructive activity) and 263 ("social change . . . comes slowly").

17. Ibid., 22.

18. Ibid., 259 ("the liberal tradition"), 131–132 ("restraint"), and 117 ("the doctrines of liberalism").

19. For a contrary understanding of Moynihan's motives for joining the Nixon White House, see Gil Troy, *Moynihan's Moment: America's Fight against Zionism as Racism* (New York: Oxford University Press, 2013), 49.

20. As will be seen, Moynihan on at least one occasion cast himself in the "center" but, crucially, as a center "liberal." That is, he saw the center-left dispute operating inside the parameters of liberal thought. See his remarks to the New York AFL-CIO, August 3, 1978, Moynihan Papers: "I won [the 1976 Democratic Senate primary] because I was able to persuade the voters that there was still [a] sound and responsible tradition of liberalism in the center of Democratic politics worthy of their support." He went on to mention "we, the forces of the liberal center."

21. For the "clown" remark, see the *Nation*, September 22, 1979. For Podhoretz, see Thomas L. Jeffers, *Norman Podhoretz: A Biography* (New York: Cambridge University Press, 2010), 192–194. For Abrams, see James Traub, "Daniel Patrick Moynihan, Liberal? Conservative? Or Just Pat?" *New York Times*, September 16, 1990, http://www.nytimes.com/books/98/10/04/specials/moynihan-mag90.html, retrieved January 29, 2014.

22. Daniel Patrick Moynihan, address at the United States Naval Academy, March 22, 1979, Moynihan Papers.

23. Todd S. Purdum, "The Newest Moynihan," *New York Times Magazine,* August 7, 1994.

24. Daniel Patrick Moynihan, *Miles to Go: A Personal History of Social Policy* (Cambridge, MA: Harvard University Press, 1996), 49.

25. Referring to the corrupting influence of supply-side ideology on the Reagan administration, which Moynihan criticized for continuing to pursue a policy of steep tax cuts and defense increases even after it was clear it was producing massive structural deficits, he wrote: "The 'science of politics' can make the demands of virtue bearable but can never substitute for them. The 1980s produced not a political crisis but an ethical one." See Moynihan, *Came the Revolution,* 321.

26. Moynihan, *Coping,* 27–28.

27. Ibid., 31. He recommended it first in print in 1973's *Coping,* and again in 1992: "We live with more troubles than we can readily endure and more demands than we can probably meet. I have long held, and say again, that there is only one political poem of the twentieth century worth remembering, Yeats' 'Parnell' in 1937"; see Daniel Patrick Moynihan, "Grey Truth: Blashfield Address," American Academy and Institute of Arts and Letters, May 20, 1992, Moynihan Papers.

CHAPTER 1: THE CENTRAL TRUTHS

1. Daniel Patrick Moynihan, "The Professionalization of Reform," *Public Interest,* no. 1 (Fall 1965): 6–16.

2. On interest group liberalism, see Theodore Lowi, *The End of Liberalism: The Second Republic of the United States* (New York: W. W. Norton, 1979). Moynihan cited it at least once, in a speech to the Democratic National Committee trustees on May 4, 1990, that he entitled "Decline and Fall?" Moynihan Papers. Moynihan was equally taken with Mancur Olson's thesis that great nations decline and fall according to the accretion of interest groups. See Olson, *The Rise and Decline of Nations: Economic Growth, Stagflation, and Social Rigidities* (New Haven, CT: Yale University Press, 1982), and Daniel Patrick Moynihan, *Counting Our Blessings: Reflections on the Future of America* (Boston: Little, Brown, 1980), 199.

3. Moynihan, *Coping,* 4.

4. Daniel Patrick Moynihan, with Suzanne Weaver, *A Dangerous Place* (Boston: Little, Brown, 1978), 17.

5. Daniel Patrick Moynihan, *The Politics of a Guaranteed Income: The Nixon*

Administration and the Family Assistance Plan (New York: Random House, 1973), 185.

6. Moynihan, *Coping,* 4–5.

7. Moynihan, *Politics of a Guaranteed Income,* 303. He continued: "By contrast, an aspect of liberal reform, as a political style, is a capacity to do large things without overmuch concern for large consequences."

8. Ibid., 352. With respect to Burke, again, at no point is the claim intellectual influence, only compatibility.

9. Moynihan, *Coping,* 257.

10. Ibid., 32–33.

11. Ibid., 255.

12. Moynihan led a yearlong Harvard faculty evaluation of the study, whose results were published in Daniel Patrick Moynihan and Frederick Mosteller, eds., *On Equality of Educational Opportunity* (New York: Vintage Books, 1972).

13. Daniel Patrick Moynihan, "Sidney Hook Memorial Award Presentation," May 3, 1996, Moynihan Papers.

14. For Coleman's despondency, see James Patterson, *Freedom Is Not Enough: The Moynihan Report and America's Struggle over Black Family Life from LBJ to Obama* (New York: Basic Books, 2010), 104.

15. Moynihan, *Maximum Feasible Misunderstanding,* 8–9. Moynihan would frequently cite the same quotation in explaining the tragedy of Vietnam.

16. Moynihan, *Counting Our Blessings,* 228–229.

17. "If politics in America is not to become the art of the impossible, the limits of politics must be perceived, and the province of moral philosophy greatly expanded," in Moynihan, *Coping,* 258. For Nisbet, see Robert Nisbet, *Twilight of Authority* (Indianapolis, IN: Liberty Fund, 2000).

18. Moynihan, *Coping,* 253.

19. Ibid. The "quest for secular grace" among the New Left also manifested in "the detestation of secular sin incarnate, namely, the United States of America."

20. Moynihan, *Counting Our Blessings,* 272.

21. Ibid., 229.

22. Daniel Patrick Moynihan, remarks, Greater Buffalo Red Cross, May 1, 1981, Moynihan Papers. Neither should Moynihan's emphasis on limitation, especially in the aftermath of the Great Society, be taken as pessimism. His disposition remained essentially cheerful, even at what were, politically, his darkest moments. *Coping* was his most overcast collection of essays, yet the introduction warned the reader of the book's "failing, and a serious one. Success is too little acknowledged." "Precious little that approaches celebration will be found in these pages. And yet how much the Nation deserves praise, and how much it needs it! To recognize and acknowledge success, however modest, is fundamen-

tal to the practice of government" (pp. 40–41). Man might be a problem-solving animal, but *homo Americanus* was a "problem-discovering one," and "in our eagerness to draw attention to problems, we do frequently tend to make them seem worse than they are. In particular we tend to depict things as worsening when in fact they are improving" (p. 280). One reason for this was the tendency of public institutions and those who benefited from them to understate the progress they had made in order to maintain their power, an insight Moynihan attributed to Norman Podhoretz (p. 39). Moynihan wrote in 1964: "Never discount the apocalyptical propensities of the expert in America. . . . [It] is nice somehow to think things are shortly going to get worse. Such anticipation sustains many an ideologue through happy times"; see his "Scrubbed Babies," April 9, 1964, an apparently unpublished manuscript in Moynihan Papers.

23. Moynihan, *Coping*, 344.

24. Moynihan, *Miles to Go*, 49. Sixteen months later, after the administration produced a 1,342-page health care bill, Republicans swept both houses of Congress in the 1994 elections.

25. Moynihan, *Maximum Feasible Misunderstanding*, 8.

26. Daniel Patrick Moynihan, statement, Hearing on Welfare Reform, May 5, 1977, Press File, Moynihan Papers.

27. Moynihan, *Coping*, 275–276. Later, early in his Senate career, Moynihan would reflect that a decade after his initial article exploring the distinction between program and policy liberalism, "the policy craze is altogether out of hand. Every other week a new national policy announces itself. In 1978, for example, a group of cabinet officers and senior officials met in the Roosevelt Room in the West Wing of the White House to begin plans for a National Cultural Policy. Go back, let us say, half a century. In what circumstances could a comparable meeting have taken place? There are but two. The first would take place in a world of imaginative satire. . . . The only other setting in which such a gathering could meet a half century ago would have been in one of the two totalitarian states: more likely Fascist Italy than Communist Russia"; see Moynihan, *Counting Our Blessings*, 270. This aside, his underlying preference for policy over program remained.

28. Moynihan, *Coping*, 382.

29. Burke, *Selected Works*, 2:93.

30. See, inter alia, Moynihan, *Counting Our Blessings*, 194–195, and Moynihan, *Came the Revolution*, xix.

31. Moynihan, *Came the Revolution*, 55.

32. Daniel Patrick Moynihan, address at Union College, June 11, 1995, Moynihan Papers. Cf. Burke.

33. Moynihan, *Coping*, 260.

34. Moynihan, *Maximum Feasible Misunderstanding*, 191.

35. Ibid., 193–194 (emphases in original).

36. Ibid., xiii.

37. Moynihan, *Coping*, 203.

38. Ibid., 180.

39. Moynihan, *Maximum Feasible Misunderstanding*, 192.

40. Moynihan, *Coping*, 267.

41. Moynihan, *Maximum Feasible Misunderstanding*, 192.

42. Moynihan, *Coping*, 267.

43. Moynihan, *Maximum Feasible Misunderstanding*, 201.

44. Moynihan, *Coping*, 190.

45. Daniel Patrick Moynihan, "President Reagan and Chairman Morrill: A Constitutional Reflection," address to the National League of Cities, March 24, 1985, Moynihan Papers.

46. For the encyclical, see http://www.vatican.va/holy_father/pius_xi/encyclicals/documents/hf_p-xi_enc_19310515_quadragesimo-anno_en.html, retrieved March 2, 2013. Moynihan quoted it, translated somewhat differently, in a September 22, 1980, address to the National Conference of Catholic Charities, Press File, Moynihan Papers. In *Beyond the Melting Pot,* Moynihan noted that *Quadragesimo Anno* and *Mater et Magistra,* both of which were critical of capitalism, committed the American church "to a social doctrine that was almost certainly far to the left of the social thinking of most American Catholics, clergy and laity alike"; see Nathan Glazer and Daniel Patrick Moynihan, *Beyond the Melting Pot: The Negroes, Puerto Ricans, Jews, Italians and Irish of New York City* (Cambridge, MA: MIT Press, 1963), 284–285.

47. Daniel Patrick Moynihan, "Soviet Ideology," remarks delivered to the Pacem in Terris IV Convocation, December 2, 1975, reprinted in *Vital Speeches of the Day,* January 1, 1976, 172–176.

48. On this point, see also Moynihan's future aide Elliot Abrams's entry in the 1976 *Commentary* symposium, entitled "What Is a Liberal—Who Is a Conservative?" Abrams argued that the primacy of individual freedom was the central liberal value and that the deflection occurred with the New Left in the 1960s; see *Commentary,* September 1976, 34–35. Similarly, Jeanne Kirkpatrick's entry identified Moynihan as an exponent of the "Left" insofar as liberalism in foreign policy meant "those who support political freedom and free emigration and oppose political imprisonment" (73).

49. Daniel Patrick Moynihan, foreword to Alva Myrdal, *Nation and Family* (Cambridge, MA: MIT Press, 1968), xi.

50. Arthur Schlesinger, "The Challenge of Abundance," *Reporter,* May 17, 1956, 8–11.

51. On this point, see Lowi, *End of Liberalism.*

52. Daniel Patrick Moynihan, *Family and Nation* (New York: Harcourt Brace Jovanovich, 1986), 79.

53. Moynihan, *Maximum Feasible Misunderstanding,* xiii (emphases in original).

54. This dichotomy is problematic with respect to what may be the Great Society's most enduring achievement, Medicare, which Moynihan warmly endorsed and which he recognized to be based on what he called "the insurance principle." Indeed, he regarded Medicare as a completion of the New Deal. The derailment of the New Deal during the Great Society occurred instead with respect to welfare. We shall explore this narrative in more detail in chapter 2, but I acknowledge at this point that it is complicated by Moynihan's initial enthusiasm for the War on Poverty.

55. The difference may be comparable to Jean-Jacques Rousseau's or Friedrich Hayek's dicta that the law must operate only at the level of generality and never take notice of specific individuals.

56. Daniel Patrick Moynihan, "Where Liberals Went Wrong," in Melvin Laird, ed., *Republican Papers* (New York: Anchor Books, 1968), 139.

57. Moynihan, *Family and Nation,* 78.

58. Moynihan, *Maximum Feasible Misunderstanding,* 193.

59. Daniel Patrick Moynihan, speech to National Coalition of Voluntary Organizations, October 4, 1978, Moynihan Papers.

60. This is precisely the sequence Tocqueville described in *Democracy in America.* See Alexis de Tocqueville, *Democracy in America,* trans. Harvey Mansfield and Delba Winthrop (Chicago: University of Chicago Press, 2002).

61. Moynihan, speech to National Coalition of Voluntary Organizations.

62. Daniel Patrick Moynihan, "Sanford Solender Lecture," United Jewish Appeal, September 14, 1987, Moynihan Papers.

63. "Conference Agrees to Revolutionary Surface Transportation Act," press release, November 26, 1991, Moynihan Papers.

64. Daniel Patrick Moynihan, remarks at 10th Anniversary of Lincoln Center Campus, Fordham University, November 14, 1979, Press File, Moynihan Papers.

65. Moynihan, *Counting Our Blessings,* 236–237.

66. Daniel Patrick Moynihan, remarks in the US Senate, August 10, 1978, Press File, Moynihan Papers.

67. Moynihan, *Counting Our Blessings,* 253.

68. Daniel Patrick Moynihan, speech entitled "On the Continuing Difficulty of Catholic Intellectual Life," May 20, 1978, Moynihan Papers.

69. Moynihan, remarks to the chief volunteer officers.

70. Moynihan, address to the National Conference of Catholic Charities.

71. Jacques Maritain, *Man and the State* (Chicago: University of Chicago Press, 1998).

72. Moynihan, address to the National Conference of Catholic Charities.

73. Daniel Patrick Moynihan, remarks in the US Senate, July 11, 1978, Moynihan Papers.

74. See Daniel Patrick Moynihan to Senator Harry Byrd, September 21, 2001, Moynihan Papers.

75. Daniel Patrick Moynihan, "Building Wealth for Everyone," *New York Times,* May 30, 2000.

76. Glazer and Moynihan, *Beyond the Melting Pot,* 290. The quotation is from the conclusion, which Moynihan wrote.

77. Daniel Patrick Moynihan, remarks to the Society of the Friendly Sons of St. Patrick 193rd Annual Dinner, March 17, 1977, Moynihan Papers.

78. Nathan Glazer and Daniel Patrick Moynihan, eds., *Ethnicity: Theory and Experience* (Cambridge, MA: Harvard University Press, 1975), 10.

79. Moynihan, *Coping,* 204–205. For his support of affirmative action, see his press statement on the *Bakke* decision, June 28, 1978, Moynihan Papers: "The point to be made about the Bakke decision is how unfortunate it is that a situation was ever allowed to develop in which so reasonable a tool as affirmative action for achieving so laudable a goal as equal opportunity for all evolved into a mechanism as crude as arbitrary quotas."

80. Moynihan, remarks to the Society of the Friendly Sons.

81. Daniel Patrick Moynihan, "Has This Country Gone Mad?" *Saturday Evening Post,* May 4, 1968. Moynihan also noted in this passage that it was "white liberal[s]" who seemed to be encouraging this violence.

82. Daniel Patrick Moynihan, ed., *On Understanding Poverty: Perspectives from the Social Sciences* (New York: Basic Books, 1969), 14–15.

83. Moynihan, *Coping,* 169–170.

84. See http://www.nixonlibrary.gov/virtuallibrary/releases/jul10/53.pdf, retrieved February 5, 2014.

85. Moynihan, *Maximum Feasible Misunderstanding,* 10. He continued: "And with Niebuhr he [Nisbet] holds that the civilization that begins by creating this autonomous individual ends by destroying him" (11). For Nisbet's analysis, see his *Quest for Community: A Study in the Ethics of Order and Freedom* (Oakland, CA: ICS Press, 1990), which cites a Moynihan jacket blurb from a previous edition: "Masterful."

86. See Nisbet, *Twilight of Authority,* and Moynihan, *Toward a National Urban Policy,* 3–4.

87. Moynihan, *Counting Our Blessings,* 38–39.

88. Ibid., 47 (emphasis in original).

89. Moynihan, *Maximum Feasible Misunderstanding*, 12.

90. Moynihan, *Coping*, 188 (emphasis in original).

91. Ibid., 197.

92. Ibid., 201.

93. Moynihan, *Family and Nation*, 32.

94. Ibid., 173–174.

95. Daniel Patrick Moynihan, "Toward a New Intolerance," *Public Interest*, no. 112 (Summer 1993): 199–122.

96. Daniel Patrick Moynihan, "The Question of the States," *Commonweal*, October 12, 1962, 65–68.

97. Moynihan, speech to National Coalition of Voluntary Organizations.

98. Daniel Patrick Moynihan, "The Third Generation and the Third Century: Choices Concerning the Quality of American Life," in Commission on Critical Choices for Americans, ed., *Qualities of Life: Critical Choices for Americans*, vol. 7 (Lexington, MA: Lexington Books, 1976), 401–464.

99. Moynihan, *Came the Revolution*, 308.

100. Ibid., 308–309.

101. Moynihan, *Coping*, 117.

102. Ibid., 236.

103. Ibid., 193.

104. Ibid., 160–161.

105. Laird, *Republican Papers*, 138. Moynihan continued: "But as an instrument for providing services, especially to urban lower-class Negroes, it is a highly unreliable device."

106. Daniel Patrick Moynihan, speech to New York County Democrats, February 19, 1981, Moynihan Papers. Moynihan's history—suggesting that the Democratic Party had, since Jefferson, stood for redistributive policies—is, of course, questionable.

107. Moynihan, *Counting Our Blessings*, 201.

108. Daniel Patrick Moynihan, commencement address, Salem College, May 8, 1977, Press File, Moynihan Papers.

109. Moynihan, *Counting Our Blessings*, 223–224.

110. Moynihan, *Family and Nation*, 190.

111. Moynihan and Mosteller, *On Equality of Educational Opportunity*, 58–59 (emphasis in original). He continued: "It is a paradoxical quality of such achievements that they are typically accompanied by intense feelings of dissatisfaction and disappointment on the part of those principally involved."

112. Moynihan, *Politics of a Guaranteed Income*, 144.

113. Daniel Patrick Moynihan, "A Return to Social Policy," speech delivered at the Conference on Setting Municipal Priorities, November 8, 1985, Moynihan Papers.

114. Moynihan, *Came the Revolution,* 289.

115. Moynihan, *Politics of a Guaranteed Income,* 14.

116. See Daniel Patrick Moynihan, statement on the takeover bid for his publisher, Harcourt Brace Jovanovich, May 22, 1987, Press File, Moynihan Papers.

117. Moynihan, *Came the Revolution,* 293–294.

118. Moynihan, speech to New York County Democrats. Some commentators have asserted Moynihan was, in fact, emphasizing his liberalism to avert a primary challenge from the left in the 1982 election. See Traub, "Daniel Patrick Moynihan, Liberal? Conservative? Or Just Pat?"

119. Moynihan, *Coping,* 23.

120. Moynihan, *Counting Our Blessings,* 197.

121. Daniel Patrick Moynihan, "Of 'Sons' and Their 'Grandsons,'" *New York Times,* July 7, 1980.

122. See Lionel Trilling, *The Liberal Imagination* (New York: New York Review of Books, 2008).

123. Moynihan, *Coping,* 131–132.

124. Laird, *Republican Papers,* 136.

125. Moynihan, *Coping,* 119.

126. Ibid., 129.

127. Ibid., 18–19.

128. Ibid., 17.

129. For treatments that describe Moynihan as a neoconservative, see, among many others, Peter Steinfels, *The Neoconservatives* (New York: Simon & Schuster, 1979); John Ehrman, *The Rise of Neoconservatism: Intellectuals and Foreign Affairs, 1945–1994* (New Haven, CT: Yale University Press, 1995); Claes Ryn, *America the Virtuous* (New Brunswick, NJ: Transaction Publishers, 2003); and Troy, *Moynihan's Moment.*

130. Daniel Patrick Moynihan, "How the Great Society 'Destroyed the American Family,'" *Public Interest,* no. 108 (Summer 1992): 53–64.

131. Moynihan, *Came the Revolution,* 201. For a recollection of Moynihan's estrangement from Norman Podhoretz, one of those to whom he seems to refer here, see Jeffers, *Norman Podhoretz.*

132. Irving Kristol, *Reflections of a Neoconservative* (New York: Basic Books, 1983), 76.

133. Steven R. Weisman, *Daniel Patrick Moynihan: A Portrait in Letters of an American Visionary* (New York: PublicAffairs, 2010), 453. At a 1997 conference honoring Moynihan, Seymour Martin Lipset said that "many of his *Public Interest* neoconfreres who have grown more conservative than he has have been unhappy with his failure to move as far as they in the same direction." See

Robert Katzmann, ed., *Daniel Patrick Moynihan: The Intellectual in Public Life* (Washington, DC: Woodrow Wilson Center Press, 1998), 41.

134. Daniel Patrick Moynihan, "Two Hundred Years of Pennsylvania Avenue," Jefferson Lecture, University of Virginia, April 13, 2000, Moynihan Papers.

135. Daniel Patrick Moynihan, "Brendan Gill and Public Architecture in New York," remarks at the National Building Museum Symposium, February 4, 1998, Moynihan Papers.

136. Daniel Patrick Moynihan, "Guiding Principles of Federal Architecture," http://www.gsa.gov/portal/content/136543, retrieved March 4, 2013.

137. Moynihan, *Coping*, 238–239.

138. Ibid., 239.

139. Daniel Patrick Moynihan, "It's a Nicer Place for a Parade Now," *Washington Post*, January 21, 1985.

140. Daniel Patrick Moynihan, "The Politics of Conservancy," lecture at the Metropolitan Museum of Art, November 7, 1984, Moynihan Papers.

141. Daniel Patrick Moynihan, foreword to Carol M. Highsmith and Ted Landphair, *Pennsylvania Avenue: America's Main Street* (Washington, DC: American Institute of Architects Press, 1988).

142. Moynihan, *Coping*, 242.

143. Ibid. (emphasis in original).

144. Daniel Patrick Moynihan, remarks in the US Senate, March 5, 1983, Moynihan Papers.

145. Daniel Patrick Moynihan, *On the Law of Nations* (Cambridge, MA: Harvard University Press, 1990), 107.

146. Ibid., 143.

147. Daniel Patrick Moynihan, Democratic Response to President's Radio Address, November 29, 1986, Press File, Moynihan Papers.

148. Daniel Patrick Moynihan, Statement on Tower Commission Report, February 26, 1987, Press File, Moynihan Papers. Significantly for appreciating Moynihan's continuing liberalism, he described the Iran contra affair as "the fruit of contempt of government"; see Moynihan, *Came the Revolution*, 185.

149. Moynihan, *Maximum Feasible Misunderstanding*, 199–200.

150. Daniel Patrick Moynihan, Statement on Supreme Court Ruling Overturning Gramm Rudman Hollings, July 7, 1986, Press File, Moynihan Papers.

151. Daniel Patrick Moynihan, remarks in the US Senate, July 31, 1986, Moynihan Papers.

152. Daniel Patrick Moynihan, remarks in the US Senate, March 27, 1996, Moynihan Papers.

153. It was also unnecessary, he argued, insofar as the deficit had at that

point been tamed, and the purportedly out-of-control deficits with which it aimed to deal were the result not of constitutional defects but of deliberate policy in the 1980s.

154. Moynihan, *Came the Revolution*, 303.

155. Daniel Patrick Moynihan, Senate Speech Supporting Bill to Repeal Line-Item Veto Act of 1996, October 24, 1997, Moynihan Papers. This presumption of conflict was also why Moynihan worried about what he dubbed the "Iron Law of Emulation"—the propensity of organizations in conflict to resemble each other—leading to the creation of "submerged horizontal bureaucracies that link the three branches of government . . . while their constitutional masters come and go"; see Moynihan, "Imperial Government," *Commentary*, June 1978, 25–32.

156. Daniel Patrick Moynihan, "The 'New Science of Politics' Vindicated, or the Founders Rediscovered," Britannica Distinguished Lecture, Woodrow Wilson Center, Washington, DC, September 12, 1986, Moynihan Papers.

157. Daniel Patrick Moynihan, remarks in the US Senate, June 27, 1979, http://teachingamericanhistory.org/library/document/statement-on-the-electoral-college/, retrieved February 14, 2014. The quotes in the next four paragraphs are all from this source.

158. For Calhoun, see his "Disquisition on Government," in Ross Lence, ed., *Union and Liberty: The Political Thought of John C. Calhoun* (Indianapolis, IN: Liberty Fund, 1992), 3–78. The actual connection between Calhoun and Moynihan's observation is tenuous; put otherwise, the similarity is arguably merely rhetorical. Calhoun's claim was that the Constitution embodied a system that gave minorities de facto veto power over the decisions of majorities, plainly not what Moynihan meant here.

159. This insight into the importance of parties as a moderating force also echoes Burke, who wrote of it in his "Thoughts on the Cause of the Present Discontents." See Edmund Burke, *Selected Works of Edmund Burke*, vol. 1, *Thoughts on the Cause of the Present Discontents and the Two Speeches on America* (Indianapolis, IN: Liberty Fund, 1999).

160. Eaton quoted in Katzmann, *Daniel Patrick Moynihan*, 150.

161. Daniel Patrick Moynihan, "We Confront, at This Very Moment, the Greatest Constitutional Crisis since the Civil War," commencement address, St. John's University Law School, June 6, 1982, Moynihan Papers. I have written elsewhere against the view Moynihan expressed in this quotation, but in the present study, I intend merely to explicate his views. See Greg Weiner, *Madison's Metronome: The Constitution, Majority Rule, and the Tempo of American Politics* (Lawrence: University Press of Kansas, 2012).

162. Daniel Patrick Moynihan, remarks in the US Senate, May 16, 1983,

Moynihan Papers. Moynihan's reverence for the courts was not blind. He extensively disparaged the Supreme Court's First Amendment jurisprudence as it applied to public funding of parochial schools, and he also warned the judiciary against venturing into social-scientific speculation. See Moynihan, *Counting Our Blessings,* chap. 8.

163. Daniel Patrick Moynihan, remarks in the US Senate, April 17, 1996, Moynihan Papers.

164. "On Values: Talking with Peggy Noonan," 1995, transcript of interview in Moynihan Papers.

165. Daniel Patrick Moynihan, remarks in the US Senate, April 25, 2000.

166. Daniel Patrick Moynihan, "Public Spending and Community," *New City,* October 1–15, 1964.

167. Moynihan, *Coping,* 363–364.

168. Daniel Patrick Moynihan, "Un-words and Policy," *New York Times,* November 21, 1978.

169. Daniel Patrick Moynihan, remarks in the US Senate, December 7, 1995, Moynihan Papers.

170. Moynihan, *Dangerous Place,* 216.

171. See Troy, *Moynihan's Moment,* 279.

CHAPTER 2: POVERTY AND PROBLEMS
POORLY STATED

1. Daniel Patrick Moynihan, "The Technological Revolution: What It Is Doing to People in Poverty," *Social Action* 13, no. 8 (April 1964): 4–13.

2. Daniel Patrick Moynihan, "Poverty and Progress," *American Scholar* 33, no. 4 (Autumn 1964): 594–606.

3. Daniel Patrick Moynihan, "America's Poor: What Is to Be Done?," address at Harvard University, September 4, 1986, Moynihan Papers.

4. See Daniel Patrick Moynihan, remarks in the US Senate, November 4, 1977, Moynihan Papers, as the Senate considered a proposal to increase Social Security benefits.

5. Daniel Patrick Moynihan, remarks in the US Senate, September 14, 1995, Moynihan Papers.

6. Moynihan, *Politics of a Guaranteed Income,* 17.

7. See, e.g., Moynihan, *Family and Nation,* 13.

8. Ibid., 23.

9. For a contrary view to that presented here, see Herbert G. Gutman, "Black History Seduced and Abandoned," *Nation,* September 22, 1979, 232–236.

10. Hodgson, *Gentleman from New York*, 135.

11. Moynihan, remarks in the US Senate, December 7, 1995.

12. Charles Murray, *Losing Ground: American Social Policy, 1950–1980* (New York: Basic Books, 1994).

13. Daniel Patrick Moynihan, statement before Select Committee on Hunger, US House, September 26, 1985, Moynihan Papers (emphasis in original).

14. Moynihan, *Family and Nation*, 135.

15. Moynihan, *Came the Revolution*, 108.

16. Moynihan, *Coping*, 349–350.

17. Moynihan, remarks at the 10th Anniversary of Lincoln Center Campus.

18. Moynihan, *Family and Nation*, 27–28.

19. Moynihan, *Miles to Go*, 222.

20. Moynihan, "Where Liberals Went Wrong," 139 ("getting more money"); Moynihan, "America's Poor" ("the clarity with which some Republicans").

21. Moynihan and Mosteller, *On Equality of Educational Opportunity*, 43. The quoted passage was jointly written with Mosteller.

22. Moynihan, *Coping*, 141–142.

23. Patterson, *Freedom Is Not Enough*, 18.

24. Moynihan, *Politics of a Guaranteed Income*, 185. Moynihan also spoke here of a hope that providing the benefit for intact families would lessen any incentives to abandon one's family in order to secure welfare.

25. Moynihan, "America's Poor."

26. Moynihan, *Family and Nation*, 69.

27. Moynihan, *Came the Revolution*, 300.

28. Moynihan, remarks in the US Senate, September 14, 1995.

29. Moynihan, *Coping*, 364.

30. Moynihan, "America's Poor."

31. See Lowi, *End of Liberalism*.

32. Moynihan, *On Understanding Poverty*, 32.

33. Moynihan, *Maximum Feasible Misunderstanding*, 179.

34. Ibid., 181–182.

35. Ibid., 187.

36. Ibid., 188.

37. Ibid., 193.

38. Moynihan, *Coping*, 361 ("except, of course," he continued parenthetically, "that the poverty level would immediately be reestimated up").

39. Ibid., 283 (emphasis in original).

40. Ibid., 377 (emphasis in original).

41. Ibid., 362.

42. Ibid., 378.

43. Lee Rainwater and William L. Yancey, *The Moynihan Report and the Politics of Controversy* (Cambridge, MA: MIT Press, 1967), 43. (Page citations for the Moynihan Report are to Rainwater and Yancey's book, where the numbers appear at the tops of the pages; because these authors reproduced a facsimile of the report, its page numbers also appear at the bottoms of the pages.)

44. Ibid., 48.

45. Ibid., 49. Later, during a 1977 commencement address, Moynihan would dismiss as "self-serving nonsense" what he characterized as Tocqueville's claim that equality was "fatal to all manner of distinctions, and perhaps first of all to those based on merit." The pressure to abolish distinctions in the 1960s had come from elites, not from below. Moreover, "if egalitarianism is deep in the American character, so is competitiveness, and so also is the desire to see the society well served"; see Moynihan, address at Colgate University, May 29, 1977, Moynihan Papers.

46. Rainwater and Yancey, *Moynihan Report,* 51.

47. Ibid., 51–52.

48. Ibid., 58.

49. Ibid., 76.

50. Ibid., 62.

51. See, for example, Christopher Jencks's critique of the report: "Moynihan's analysis is in the conservative tradition. . . . The guiding assumption is that the social pathology is caused less by basic defects in the social system than by defects in particular individuals and groups which prevent their adjusting to the system"; quoted in Patterson, *Freedom Is Not Enough,* 78. This was, of course, precisely the reverse of what Moynihan had said. For another critique of the report, this one arguing that Moynihan's error was projecting the power dynamics of white families onto African American ones, see Charles V. Willie and Susan L. Greenblatt, "Four 'Classic' Studies of Power Relationships in Black Families: A Review and Look to the Future," *Journal of Marriage and Family* 40, no. 4 (November 1978): 691–694.

52. Moynihan, *Coping,* 21.

53. Rainwater and Yancey, *Moynihan Report,* 75.

54. Ibid.

55. Daniel Patrick Moynihan, "Defining Deviancy Down," *American Scholar* 62, no. 1 (Winter 1993): 17–31 (the phrase "task *overload*" is Moynihan quoting Deborah A. Dawson).

56. "On Values: Talking with Peggy Noonan." I have corrected the verbal slips in the original transcript, in which Moynihan said, "We have lost a family structure capable of, of disciplining young males. It is the, the most difficult thing in any society."

57. Rainwater and Yancey, *Moynihan Report*, 81.

58. Ibid., 93.

59. Ibid.

60. Ibid., 94.

61. Lyndon B. Johnson, "To Fulfill These Rights," June 4, 1965, http://www.lbjlib.utexas.edu/johnson/archives.hom/speeches.hom/650604.asp, retrieved June 21, 2013.

62. Daniel Patrick Moynihan, "A Family Policy for the Nation," *America* 113, no. 12 (September 4, 1965): 280–283.

63. Ibid.

64. Moynihan's foreword to Myrdal, *Nation and Family*, x (emphasis in original).

65. Johnson, "To Fulfill These Rights," 2.

66. Myrdal, *Nation and Family*, xv.

67. Moynihan, *Family and Nation*, 10.

68. Moynihan, *Politics of a Guaranteed Income*, 25.

69. Ibid., 21.

70. Myrdal, *Nation and Family*, xv–xvi.

71. Moynihan, "Family Policy."

72. Rainwater and Yancey, *Moynihan Report*, 67.

73. Myrdal, *Nation and Family*, xii.

74. Daniel Patrick Moynihan, "Toward a Post-industrial Social Policy," *Public Interest*, no. 96 (Summer 1989): 16–27. For the Dahrendorf essay, which Moynihan quoted several times, see "On the Origins of Inequality among Men," in Ralf Dahrendorf, *Essays in the Theory of Society* (Stanford, CA: Stanford University Press, 1968), 151–178.

75. Moynihan, *Miles to Go*, 221.

76. See, for example, Troy, *Moynihan's Moment*, and Traub, "Daniel Patrick Moynihan, Liberal? Conservative? Or Just Pat?"

77. Moynihan, *Politics of a Guaranteed Income*, 131–132. His diagnosis of the problem was that "the prolonged absence of serious political and intellectual opposition was in the end deeply debilitating" to Democrats.

78. Katzmann, *Daniel Patrick Moynihan*, 173.

79. Moynihan, *Toward a National Urban Policy*, 20 (emphases in original).

80. Moynihan, *Coping*, 75 (emphases in original).

81. Moynihan and Mosteller, *On Equality of Educational Opportunity*, 50.

82. For his support in 1964, see Patterson, *Freedom Is Not Enough*, 20. Patterson emphasized that Moynihan was clearly thinking early in terms of family rather than individual policy. He also emphasized other policies such as the availability of birth control.

83. Moynihan, *Politics of a Guaranteed Income,* 160.

84. Ibid., 223. For the phase-out level, see p. 230. For the federal poverty rate in 1969, see http://www.ssa.gov/history/fisheronpoverty.html, retrieved February 27, 2014.

85. Moynihan, *Coping,* 160–161.

86. Moynihan, *Politics of a Guaranteed Income,* 50.

87. Ibid., 147–148 (emphases in original).

88. Ibid., 139.

89. Ibid., 138.

90. Ibid., 549–550.

91. Moynihan, "America's Poor."

92. As will be seen, Moynihan later revisited this conclusion.

93. Moynihan, *Politics of a Guaranteed Income,* 7.

94. Ibid., 4 ("it was not accompanied") and 317–318 ("in effect the public asked").

95. See Daniel Patrick Moynihan to William F. Buckley, printed in the *National Review,* September 29, 1978, 1196. For Moynihan's reaction to the SIME-DIME experiments, see also Brian Steensland, *The Failed Welfare Revolution: America's Struggle over Guaranteed Income Policy* (Princeton, NJ: Princeton University Press, 2008), 215, and Glazer, *Limits of Social Policy,* 30–31. The SIME-DIME experiments have been the subject of intense debate as to statistical interpretation. (See, for example, note 21 in chapter 4.) Other critics of Moynihan, such as Philip Green, have pointed with approval to the results, suggesting that income transfers empowered women to leave already unstable marriages. See Green, "The Wayward Social Scientist," *Nation,* September 22, 1979, 231–232.

96. Daniel Patrick Moynihan, statement to House Special Subcommittee on Welfare Reform, September 30, 1977, Moynihan Papers.

97. Press release, June 28, 1978, Moynihan Papers.

98. See the editorial entitled "A 'No Frills' Welfare Dilemma," *New York Times,* July 5, 1978, and Cloward and Piven, "Welfare Vaudevillian," 236–239. The Cloward-Piven piece, part of a bitter, issue-long broadside against Moynihan—then rumored as a potential primary challenger to President Carter in 1980 despite his denials of any such ambition—also accused him of misusing social science, among other charges.

99. Daniel Patrick Moynihan, "One Third of a Nation," *New Republic,* June 9, 1982, 18–21.

100. Daniel Patrick Moynihan, "A Return to Social Policy," speech at the Conference on Setting Municipal Priorities, Harriman, NY, November 8, 1985. Poverty had also not won insofar as Social Security and Medicare had dramatically reduced poverty among the elderly: "If one sees the 1960s and early 1970s

as the culmination of a long effort, beginning in the Progressive era, to eliminate the particular kinds of poverty and distress associated with industrialism,
there were hugely successful years. The effort was not, however, successful in
dealing with an emergent form of dependency and difficulty which I associate
with postindustrial society"; see Moynihan, *Miles to Go*, 215.

101. "Moynihan Introduces Bill to Stop Welfare Benefit Cuts," press release,
October 16, 1987, Moynihan Papers ("terminal sleaze"), and Moynihan, *Family
and Nation*, 68–69 ("there is no question").

102. The one fault Moynihan did lay at the feet of the Great Society was its
having given "great influence in social policy to viewpoints that rejected the
proposition that family structure might be a social issue. Accordingly, even if
social policy might have produced some effective responses, no such responses
were attempted"; see Moynihan, "How the Great Society 'Destroyed the American Family.'"

103. Moynihan, *Came the Revolution*, 104.

104. Daniel Patrick Moynihan, "Half the Nation's Children: Born without a
Fair Chance," *New York Times*, September 25, 1988.

105. Daniel Patrick Moynihan, remarks in the US Senate, January 28, 1988,
Moynihan Papers.

106. Daniel Patrick Moynihan, remarks in the US Senate, July 31, 1992,
Moynihan Papers.

107. Daniel Patrick Moynihan, "A Landmark for Families," *New York Times*,
November 16, 1992, Moynihan Papers.

108. Moynihan, remarks in the US Senate, September 14, 1995. Moynihan em-
ployed similar refrains elsewhere. In reality, Reagan had proposed turning welfare
wholly over to the states, at which point Moynihan responded that Eisenhower
would have done no such thing. See Moynihan, *Family and Nation*, 68.

109. Moynihan, remarks in the US Senate, September 14, 1995.

110. Ibid.

111. Daniel Patrick Moynihan, remarks in the US Senate, December 27, 1995,
Moynihan Papers.

112. Moynihan, remarks in the US Senate, December 7, 1995, draft of floor
statement, in Moynihan Papers.

113. Moynihan, remarks in the US Senate, September 14, 1995. Moynihan
continued: "One group was in Washington yesterday and I can speak with some
spirit on that. This was a group of Catholic bishops and members from Catholic Charities. They were here. They were in Washington. Nobody else. None of
the great marchers, the great chanters, the nonnegotiable demanders."

114. Daniel Patrick Moynihan, "Statement Concerning the Administration
Report on the Welfare Repeal Legislation," November 9, 1995 ("bartering");

Moynihan, remarks in the US Senate, September 8, 1995 ("sleeping on grates"); Moynihan, remarks in the US House-Senate conference on welfare reform, October 24, 1995 ("infants put to the sword"). All are in Moynihan Papers.

115. Daniel Patrick Moynihan, Timothy M. Smeeding, and Lee Rainwater, eds., *The Future of the Family* (New York: Russell Sage Foundation, 2006), 15.

116. Stephanie J. Ventura, "Changing Patterns of Nonmarital Childbearing in the United States," National Center for Health Statistics Data Brief no. 18, May 2009, http://www.cdc.gov/nchs/data/databriefs/db18.pdf, retrieved December 26, 2013.

117. Moynihan, *Coping*, 164.

118. Daniel Patrick Moynihan, remarks in the US Senate Finance Committee hearing, February 22, 1996, Moynihan Papers.

119. Moynihan, Smeeding, and Rainwater, *Future of the Family*, xxi.

120. Ibid., 15.

121. See https://www.census.gov/prod/2013pubs/p60-245.pdf, p. 15, retrieved February 14, 2014. The figures indicate that child poverty rates did continue to decline after the passage of welfare reform that had begun with the economic expansion of 1992 and 1993. They began to rise again in approximately 2000.

122. Moynihan, remarks in the US Senate, September 14, 1995.

123. Moynihan, *Miles to Go*, 230.

124. Moynihan, "Toward a Post-industrial Social Policy," 19.

125. Ibid., 24.

126. For an illustrative critique, see Andrew Karmen, "'Defining Deviancy Down': How Senator Moynihan's Misleading Phrase about Criminal Justice Is Rapidly Being Incorporated into Popular Culture," *Journal of Criminal Justice and Popular Culture* 2, no. 5 (1994): 99–112, http://www.albany.edu/scj/jcjpc/vol2is5/deviancy.html, retrieved January 20, 2014.

127. Moynihan, "Defining Deviancy Down," 19.

128. Ibid., 21.

129. Ibid., 22.

130. Moynihan was not above making this claim himself. A 1991 press release read, "Underfunding Head Start means shortchanging our future"; see "Full Funding of Head Start Urged by Sen. Moynihan," April 18, 1991, Moynihan Papers.

131. Moynihan, "Defining Deviancy Down," 23 (emphasis in original).

132. Ibid., 25–26.

133. Ibid., 26–27.

134. Ibid., 30.

135. "Moynihan Introduces Family Enhancement Legislation," press release and statement, September 25, 1998, Moynihan Papers.

136. Moynihan, Smeedling, and Rainwater, *Future of the Family*, xxi. This es-

say was edited and, after Moynihan's death, amended by Timothy M. Smeeding. Moynihan also coauthored a chapter in this volume with Smeeding and Lee Rainwater.

137. Ibid., xxii.

138 Ibid., xxiv.

CHAPTER 3: THE UNITED STATES IN ASPIRATION

1. Kathleen Teltsch, "Moynihan Calls on U.S. to 'Start Raising Hell' in U.N.," *New York Times,* February 26, 1975, 3.

2. Katzmann, *Daniel Patrick Moynihan,* 130.

3. Daniel Patrick Moynihan, address to the Council on Foreign Relations, February 14, 1979, Moynihan Papers.

4. Moynihan, *Dangerous Place,* 27.

5. Daniel Patrick Moynihan, remarks in the US Senate, March 4, 1977, Moynihan Papers.

6. See, for example, Moynihan's self-description in a statement to *The New Republic* on October 31, 1977, in Moynihan Papers: "I'm a member of the [Americans for Democratic Action] generation: people who got out of the services after the Second World War and wanted to get into liberal politics.

In New York, and I expect a lot of other places, the central struggle of the time was with the Stalinist left. ADA organized us, and upheld us."

7. Daniel Patrick Moynihan, "The United States in Opposition," *Commentary,* March 1, 1975, http://www.commentarymagazine.com/article/the-united -states-in-opposition/, retrieved January 24, 2014. All references to the essay are to the online version and hence are not paginated; in quoted lines from this document, emphases are in the original.

8. See Moynihan, *Dangerous Place,* 35.

9. Ibid., 160. For a narrative of the speech and its aftermath, see Troy, *Moynihan's Moment,* 101–105.

10. Ibid., 162–163.

11. Ibid., 168.

12. Ibid., 236–237.

13. Ibid., 237–238. Moynihan quoted here a passage from Leo Strauss, who endorsed "a society with frontiers, a closed society, concerned with self-improvement."

14. Ibid., 270.

15. Ibid., 270–271.

16. Moynihan, *Counting Our Blessings*, 101 (emphasis added).

17. Paul Warnke, "Apes on a Treadmill," *Foreign Policy*, no. 18 (Spring 1975): 12–29.

18. Moynihan, remarks in the US Senate, March 4, 1977.

19. Excerpted in Moynihan's "Reflections on United States Foreign Policy," US Senate, January 10, 1980, Moynihan Papers.

20. Moynihan, address at United States Naval Academy.

21. Daniel Patrick Moynihan, *Loyalties* (New York: Harcourt Brace Jovanovich, 1984), 17.

22. Daniel Patrick Moynihan, speech to the conference on "The Future of the Democratic Party," September 6, 1984, Moynihan Papers. The address, which is in Moynihan's speech file, is unlabeled but contains a reference to the meeting having this title.

23. Daniel Patrick Moynihan, *Pandaemonium: Ethnicity in International Politics* (New York: Oxford University Press, 1993), 38.

24. Moynihan, commencement address, University of Arkansas.

25. Daniel Patrick Moynihan, "Will Russia Blow Up?" *Newsweek*, November 19, 1979, 144. For Hodgson, see his *Gentleman from New York*, 283.

26. Moynihan, "Reflections on United States Foreign Policy."

27. Katzmann, *Daniel Patrick Moynihan*, 138.

28. Moynihan, *Pandaemonium*, 41.

29. Daniel Patrick Moynihan, commencement address, New York University, May 24, 1984, Moynihan Papers. The conviction had deepened by that October, when he said at a news conference: "There is a basic fact, so elemental, why do we have difficulty understanding it: The Cold War is over. The West won. . . . The Soviet Union is a failed society and an unstable one. . . . The place has collapsed. As a society, it just doesn't work. Nobody believes in it anymore." See Moynihan, *Came the Revolution*, 43.

30. This was the title of chapter 2 of *A Dangerous Place*, which, coyly, answered the question only obliquely. See Moynihan, *Dangerous Place*, 16–38.

31. Moynihan, *Counting Our Blessings*, 7–8.

32. Ibid., 8.

33. Ibid., 11.

34. Daniel Patrick Moynihan, commencement address, Syracuse University College of Law, May 13, 1984, Moynihan Papers.

35. Moynihan, *On the Law of Nations*, 102.

36. Edmund Burke, *Selected Works of Edmund Burke*, vol. 3, *Letters on a Regicide Peace* (Indianapolis, IN: Liberty Fund, 1999), 124.

37. Peter J. Stanlis, "Edmund Burke and the Law of Nations," *American Journal of International Law* 47, no. 3 (July 1953): 400.

38. Moynihan's position resembles the distinction Raymond Aron, whom he admired, drew between the "morality of law," on the one hand, and the "morality of struggle," on the other—with the "morality of prudence" superseding both. See Aron, *Peace and War: A Theory of International Relations* (New Brunswick, NJ: Transaction Publishers, 2003), 608–610.

39. Moynihan, address to the Council on Foreign Relations. Wilson was a great admirer of Burke, as well, but also arguably misperceived his character, underscoring the latter's reformist credentials but underemphasizing his conservatism. The two qualities are, of course, entirely compatible.

40. Moynihan, *Pandaemonium*, 147. For Iklé, see Moynihan, "Un-words and Policy."

41. Moynihan, *Counting Our Blessings*, 13–14.

42. Ibid., 14–15.

43. Significantly, Moynihan noted, although religious belief had leached out of international affairs among elites, the one institution that clung to Wilsonian beliefs in this regard was organized labor.

44. Moynihan, *Counting Our Blessings*, 17–18.

45. Ibid., 20.

46. Moynihan, *Dangerous Place*, 269.

47. Moynihan, *Counting Our Blessings*, 21. For the full discussion of the issue encapsulated here, see pp. 19–21.

48. Moynihan, *Loyalties*, 69. For Wilson's Anglophilia and its influence on the American entry into World War I, see Moynihan, *Pandaemonium*, 14.

49. Moynihan, *On the Law of Nations*, 44.

50. Ibid., 99–100.

51. Moynihan, *Loyalties*, 74–75.

52. Moynihan, *On the Law of Nations*, 174.

53. Daniel Patrick Moynihan, remarks in the US Senate, July 11, 1985, Moynihan Papers.

54. Daniel Patrick Moynihan, "The United States and the International Labor Organization: 1889–1934" (Ph.D. diss., Tufts University, 1960), 2–3.

55. Daniel Patrick Moynihan, remarks in the US Senate, September 21, 1990, Moynihan Papers.

56. Moynihan, *On the Law of Nations*, 119.

57. Ibid., 7.

58. Ibid., 129.

59. Ibid., 128. Moynihan advised a similar reaction to communism in Managua. See Daniel Patrick Moynihan, *Secrecy: The American Experience* (New Haven, CT: Yale University Press, 1998), 207–208.

60. Moynihan, *On the Law of Nations*, 131.

61. Ibid., 132. Moynihan acknowledged that exigent situations naturally arose, in international as in domestic law, in which it had to be suspended for the greater good.

62. Ibid., 133–134.

63. Moynihan, remarks in the US Senate, July 11, 1985.

64. Moynihan, *Loyalties*, 65 (emphasis in original). In a Senate speech, he quoted James Reston of the *New York Times*: "What if everybody acted on this idea? Why should the United States support this vicious notion, so central to Soviet policy? And why did President Reagan defend the right of nations to do anything they pleased if their own interests were at stake?"; Daniel Patrick Moynihan, remarks in the US Senate, November 3, 1983, Moynihan Papers.

65. Moynihan, *On the Law of Nations*, 143.

66. Ibid., 148–149.

67. Ibid., 7–8. For the twentieth century as a struggle between the Wilsonian and Leninist visions, see p. 33.

68. Daniel Patrick Moynihan, remarks in the US Senate, July 10, 1996, Moynihan Papers. Moynihan continued: "Gorbachev knew what it meant for the Soviets to assert that they would be bound by norms of international law. Quite simply, official Washington did not, for it no longer actively felt that the United States was bound by such norms."

69. Daniel Patrick Moynihan, remarks in the US Senate, August 2, 1990, Moynihan Papers (emphasis in original).

70. Ibid.

71. Moynihan, *Pandaemonium*, 9.

72. Moynihan, *On the Law of Nations*, 155.

73. Moynihan, remarks in the US Senate, August 2, 1990.

74. Hodgson, *Gentleman from New York*, 329.

75. Daniel Patrick Moynihan, remarks in the US Senate, January 12, 1991, Moynihan Papers (emphases in original).

76. Daniel Patrick Moynihan, "Next Step in the Gulf—It's Almost Midnight; Restraint, Mr. Bush," *New York Times*, January 15, 1991.

77. Moynihan, remarks in the US Senate, January 12, 1991.

78. See http://daccess-dds-ny.un.org/doc/RESOLUTION/GEN/NR0/575/28/ IMG/NR057528.pdf?OpenElement, retrieved February 2, 2014.

79. Daniel Patrick Moynihan, remarks in the US Senate, May 3, 1999, Moynihan Papers.

80. Moynihan, *Counting Our Blessings*, 19.

81. Moynihan, *Pandaemonium*, 97 (emphasis in original).

82. Moynihan, *On the Law of Nations*, 157–158.

83. Moynihan, "Grey Truth."

84. Moynihan, *Pandaemonium,* 158.

85. Ibid., 145–146.

86. Moynihan, *On the Law of Nations,* 13.

87. Moynihan, *Pandaemonium,* 168–169.

88. Ibid., 173.

89. Ibid., 173–174.

90. Daniel Patrick Moynihan, address to the National Press Club, June 5, 1992, Moynihan Papers.

91. Daniel Patrick Moynihan, "Our Stupid but Permanent CIA: What Are We Going to Do about It?" *Washington Post,* July 24, 1994.

92. Moynihan, *Pandaemonium,* 23.

93. Moynihan, *Secrecy,* 59.

94. Ibid., 70–74.

95. Daniel Patrick Moynihan, "The Potemkin Palace," address to United States Military Academy, October 4, 1985, Moynihan Papers.

96. Moynihan, *Secrecy,* 79.

97. Moynihan, "Our Stupid but Permanent CIA" (capitalization in original).

98. John Judis, "The Case for Abolishing the CIA," http://carnegieendow ment.org/2005/12/20/case-for-abolishing-cia/1yxo, retrieved February 4, 2014.

99. Moynihan, *Secrecy,* 217.

100. Ibid., 221–222.

101. Moynihan, remarks in the US Senate, July 11, 1985.

102. Moynihan, *Secrecy,* 207–208.

103. Daniel Patrick Moynihan, "Ethnicity Now," *Washington Post,* September 16, 2001.

104. Moynihan, remarks in the US Senate, April 17, 1996.

105. Daniel Patrick Moynihan, address at Union College, June 11, 1995, Moynihan Papers (emphasis in original).

106. Ibid.

107. Moynihan, "Two Hundred Years of Pennsylvania Avenue."

108. Daniel Patrick Moynihan, "Principles of Liberty," *Washington Post,* February 3, 2003.

CHAPTER 4: TOWARD A BURKEAN LIBERALISM

1. Daniel Patrick Moynihan, remarks in the US Senate, February 4, 1994, Moynihan Papers.

2. Daniel Patrick Moynihan, "Educational Goals and Political Plans," *Public*

Interest, no. 102 (Winter 1991): 32–48. In a broader sense, Moynihan believed the War on Poverty could have benefited from a deficiency model with respect to income, but that was because the problem in that case *was* demonstrably deficiency.

3. Moynihan, *Toward a National Urban Policy,* 11.

4. Burke, *Selected Works,* 2:153.

5. Ibid., 2:272.

6. Moynihan, *Coping,* 254. See Michael Polanyi, *Beyond Nihilism* (New York: Cambridge University Press, 1960), 20.

7. Moynihan, "On the Exhaustion of Political Ideas."

8. Katzmann, *Daniel Patrick Moynihan,* 175.

9. Burke, *Selected Works,* 2:272.

10. Ibid., 2:122.

11. Moynihan, *Coping,* 43. He noted in the same essay: "Norman Podhoretz has done us all a service by pointing to the unvarying political content of the proclamation of impending doom. The person making such a statement is asking that power someone else has be given to him or to her."

12. Moynihan and Mosteller, *On Equality of Educational Opportunity,* 12 (acknowledging progress), and Moynihan, *Coping,* 249 ("What then. . . .").

13. Edmund Burke, "Speech on Conciliation with the Colonies," in Burke, *Selected Works* 1:279. Moynihan once quoted Burke's companion "Speech on American Taxation." See Moynihan, *Came the Revolution,* 71.

14. Burke, *Selected Works,* 2:124.

15. Moynihan, *Coping,* 30.

16. Moynihan, *Politics of a Guaranteed Income,* 352.

17. Edmund Burke, "An Appeal from the New to the Old Whigs," in Daniel E. Ritchie, ed., *Further Reflections on the Revolution in France* (Indianapolis, IN: Liberty Fund, 1992), 91.

18. Moynihan, *Coping,* 263.

19. Moynihan, *Counting Our Blessings,* 330.

20. Moynihan, *Politics of a Guaranteed Income,* 444. "Certainly," reads the preceding line, "the idea of limits was not much in fashion," and Moynihan continued after: "This was a time of expressive politics. Anyone who asked what would follow this or that grand gesture—unilateral withdrawal from Vietnam, a $3,600 or $5,500, or $6,500 guaranteed income—was likely to be charged with opposing the ends as well as the means."

21. Glen G. Cain and Douglas A. Wissoker, "A Reanalysis of Marital Stability in the Seattle-Denver Income-Maintenance Experiment," *American Journal of Sociology* 95, no. 5 (March 1990): 1235–1269.

22. For a discussion of Burke's views on the topic, see Yuval Levin, *The Great*

Debate: Edmund Burke, Thomas Paine, and the Birth of Right and Left (New York: Basic Books, 2014), 116–125.

23. Daniel Patrick Moynihan, remarks in the US Senate, August 1, 1996, Moynihan Papers.

24. Moynihan, *Maximum Feasible Misunderstanding*, 193 (emphasis in original).

25. Burke, *Selected Works*, 2:191.

26. Michael Oakeshott, *Rationalism in Politics* (Indianapolis, IN: Liberty Fund, 1991), 7.

27. Burke, *Selected Works*, 2:193.

28. Ibid., 191.

29. Moynihan, *Maximum Feasible Misunderstanding*, 202. See Burke, *Selected Works*, 2:121.

30. Burke, *Selected Works*, 2:121–122.

31. Cf. Bertrand de Jouvenel's "myth of the solution": "The assumption that political problems are of the same kind as those set to us in the classroom, or as those which exercise the minds of geometricians, is optimistic insofar as it carries the implication that there is a right answer to every problem." But "what constitutes 'a political problem' is the clashing of terms, that is, its unsolvability." See Jouvenel, *The Pure Theory of Politics* (Indianapolis, IN: Liberty Fund, 2000), 267 and 269.

32. Nisbet, *Quest for Community*, 240.

33. Daniel Patrick Moynihan, "One Third of a Nation—Still," Bruno Lecture, November 5, 1981, Speech File, Moynihan Papers. For Coleman on "microstructures," see Moynihan's speech to the Annual Meeting and Dinner of the Associated YM-YWHAs of Greater New York, October 9, 1984, Moynihan Papers.

34. The first quotation is from US Senate debate on January 25, 1979, Moynihan Papers. The context is Moynihan's attempt, with Senator Bob Packwood, to expand the tax deductibility of charitable donations to taxpayers who did not otherwise itemize. The second is from a speech to the Greater Buffalo Red Cross, May 1, 1981, Moynihan Papers.

35. Moynihan, *Dangerous Place*, 160.

36. Moynihan, *Toward a National Urban Policy*, 3–4.

37. Burke, *Selected Works*, 2:136.

38. Moynihan, remarks to the chief volunteer officers.

39. Moynihan, speech to the Annual Meeting and Dinner of the Associated YM-YWHAs.

40. Moynihan, address to the National Conference of Catholic Charities. Moynihan said: "One cannot, for example, readily imagine case assistance to the

poor, the unemployed, the elderly and the disabled being provided as a matter of right other than by the state."

41. Moynihan, remarks to the chief volunteer officers.

42. Moynihan, *Dangerous Place,* 160.

43. Moynihan, *Family and Nation,* 193.

44. Edmund Burke, *Further Reflections on the Revolution in France* (Indianapolis, IN: Liberty Fund, 1992), 13–14.

45. Daniel Patrick Moynihan, "Additional Views of Senator Daniel Patrick Moynihan to the Annual Report of the Senate Select Committee on Intelligence," May 18, 1977, Moynihan Papers. In the press release, it is rendered, "Fiat justicia et ruant coeli."

46. Daniel Patrick Moynihan, remarks in the US Senate, September 3, 1998, Moynihan Papers.

47. Burke, *Selected Works,* 2:93.

48. Ibid., 3:144.

49. Moynihan, *Coping,* 29–30 (emphasis in original).

50. Ibid., 29.

51. See Hodgson, *Gentleman from New York,* 154–155.

52. Moynihan, "'New Science of Politics' Vindicated."

53. Moynihan, *Coping,* 244.

54. Ibid., 257–258.

55. Burke, *Selected Works,* 3:68–69.

56. Moynihan, *Coping,* 13.

Suggestions for Further Reading

The reader interested in Moynihan as a political *thinker*—as opposed to Moynihan as a political actor or political commentator—will find a paucity of secondary literature. The two most worthwhile works specifically on Moynihan are Godfrey Hodgson's *The Gentleman from New York: Daniel Patrick Moynihan, a Biography* (New York: Houghton Mifflin, 2000), the most comprehensive personal and intellectual biography available, and Robert A. Katzmann's *Daniel Patrick Moynihan: The Intellectual in Public Life* (Washington, DC: Woodrow Wilson Center Press, 1998), a Festschrift featuring essays from many of Moynihan's closest friends, collaborators, and admirers. Steven R. Weisman's *Daniel Patrick Moynihan: A Portrait in Letters of an American Visionary* (New York: PublicAffairs, 2010) contains both an excellent introductory essay and a lively and engaging collection of letters and memoranda. For reasons explained in the preface, I have generally not relied on these sources here, but readers seeking a comprehensive portrait of both the public and the private man will find them indispensable.

For treatments of specific periods or issues, James Patterson's *Freedom Is Not Enough: The Moynihan Report and America's Struggle over Black Family Life—From LBJ to Obama* (New York: Basic Books, 2010), which deals with the Moynihan Report and Moynihan's subsequent work on welfare and the family, supplies an excellent and analytically rich portrait of both Moynihan's crucible and the nation's ongoing effort to grapple with the issues he raised. Gil Troy's *Moynihan's Moment: America's Fight against Zionism as Racism* (New York: Oxford University Press, 2013) details his fight against the Zionism-as-racism resolution, and though I disagree with its portrayal of Moynihan as a neoconservative, it both makes a compelling argument that deserves a hearing and provides an excellent and thorough account of a pivotal period in Moynihan's career.

Moynihan's own writings are voluminous. Most of his books, sadly, are out of print. But teachers wishing to introduce students to his political thought may find several writings accessible and illuminating. None is more revealing than the long introduction to *Coping: On the Practice of Government* (New York: Random House, 1973). Moynihan comes closer here than anywhere else to delineating a systematic theory of politics. It is, of course, the product of a moment in time at which the theme of limitation occupied the forefront of Moynihan's mind, but my contention is that this remained a consistent commitment. *The Politics of a Guaranteed Income: The Nixon Administration and the Family Assistance Plan* (New York: Random House, 1973) is outwardly a memoir, technically a case study, and at moments an exercise in political theorizing about that of which government is capable. These insights, as is the case throughout Moynihan's writings, are sprinkled throughout the book rather than being concentrated in any one place (hence the value of the introduction to *Coping*).

"A Family Policy for the Nation," published in the liberal Catholic journal *America* (September 4, 1965), shows the early emergence of Moynihan's commitment to family and some of his first published warnings about the sociological and political consequences of its decline. His brief foreword to the 1967 edition of Alva Myrdal's *Nation and Family,* to whose reprinting Moynihan was essential, is theoretically rich on the same topic. *Maximum Feasible Misunderstanding,* again outwardly a memoir and nominally a case study—this one of the War on Poverty's community action programs—contains several reflections on the nature of politics and of government's obligations.

His June 1978 essay "Imperial Government" (*Commentary*) forecasts a process of "competitive emulation" whereby bureaucracies will become entrenched and subvert democratic governance. On October 4 of that year, his speech to the Coalition of National Voluntary Organizations, available in the Moynihan Papers at the Library of Congress, provides a deep reflection on subsidiarity. *A Dangerous Place* (Boston: Little, Brown, 1978), cowritten with his aide Suzanne Weaver (now Garment), contains an introductory memoir and a portrait of Moynihan during a period that demanded the defense of absolute values. Moynihan's Senate floor speech defending the Electoral College on June 27, 1979, is perhaps his longest and deepest sustained reflection on the political theory of the Constitution. His remarks before the United Way in New York City (on July 23, 1979), with which this book opens and also in the Moynihan Papers at the Library of Congress, are wonderfully reflective on the proper balance between government and subsidiary institutions; so is his speech at Fordham University on November 14 of that year.

Moynihan's lengthy "Reflections on United States Foreign Policy," inserted into the *Congressional Record* on January 10, 1980, marks one of his first public statements of his then-emergent view that the Soviet implosion was, if not imminent, at least visible on the horizon. His 1980 collection *Counting Our Blessings: Reflections on the Future of America* (Boston: Little, Brown, 1980) explores his views on Woodrow Wilson, international law, and the foreign policy of the Carter administration, among other topics. It also contains an essay on the proper uses of social science: retrospective rather than prospective.

His May 1, 1981, remarks to the Greater Buffalo Chapter of the American

Red Cross (Moynihan Papers) are vintage Moynihan, which is to say this was a simple, out-of-the-way speech, delivered to an audience that surely expected little more than glad-handing, that turned into a searching reflection on the place of voluntary organizations in the American regime. A commencement address at New York University on May 24, 1984 (Moynihan Papers), delineates his view, contained in his closing punch line, that the United States should "wait out" the Soviet Union. The slender volume *Loyalties* (New York: Harcourt Brace Jovanovich, 1984) deals in sequence with the MX missile's alteration of the US nuclear posture, the persistent anti-Zionist and anti-Western activities of the Soviet Union, and the importance of international law.

"The Potemkin Palace," delivered on October 4, 1985 (Sol Feinstein Lecture, Moynihan Papers), illustrates Moynihan's futile efforts both to warn of the impending Soviet collapse and to argue that a continuing and hugely expensive American military buildup was unnecessary. Another speech, September 4, 1986's "America's Poor: What Is to Be Done?" (John F. Kennedy School of Government, Moynihan Papers), recalls the early days of the War on Poverty, refutes the argument that it caused social pathologies, and pleads for a social policy "with a little more feeling." His Godkin Lectures, published in 1986 as *Family and Nation* (San Diego, CA: Harcourt Brace Jovanovich), exhaustively detail his history on the issue of poverty and his thoughts about it—although they are rarely explicitly prescriptive—going forward. *Came the Revolution: Argument in the Reagan Era* (San Diego, CA: Harcourt Brace Jovanovich, 1988) is a collection of speeches and essays detailing his rhetorical combat with the Republican orthodoxies of the 1980s, a period when Moynihan went into opposition.

His *New York Times* op-ed "Another War—the One on Poverty—Is Over, Too" (July 16, 1990) laments the petering out of antipoverty efforts after the fiscal exhaustion of the Cold War, illustrating Moynihan's persistent commitment to the issue. His Senate speeches in 1990 and 1991 on the Iraqi invasion of Kuwait and the US response—on August 2 and September 21, 1990, and January 12, 1991—show the complexities of his views of international law at the moment of its seeming post–Cold War resurgence. So does his propitiously timed volume *On the Law of Nations* (Cambridge, MA: Harvard University Press, 1990). "Defining Deviancy Down" (*American Scholar*, Winter 1993) was a landmark essay of the sort that would have been a mark of distinction for any scholar, senator or not. Its entry into the lexicon is testament to its influence. *Pandaemonium: Ethnicity in International Politics* (Oxford: Oxford University Press, 1993) marked, perhaps, a low point in Moynihan's intellectual relationship with Woodrow Wilson, even as he retained his faith in Wilson's regime of international law to mitigate ethnic tensions.

Moynihan delivered a raft of alternately poignant, passionate, and acerbic

floor statements on welfare reform in 1995 and 1996. The best of these are excerpted in *Miles to Go: A Personal History of Social Policy* (Cambridge, MA: Harvard University Press, 1996). *Secrecy: The American Experience* (New Haven, CT:
Yale University Press, 1998) is a rich historical and contemporary analysis of the
culture of secrecy that enveloped Washington during the Cold War and persisted after it. His public reflections on 9/11 and its aftermath include the *Washington Post* op-eds "Ethnicity Now" (September 16, 2001) and "Principles of
Liberty" (February 3, 2003). Moynihan died in March 2003. His edited volume
The Future of the Family (New York: Russell Sage Foundation, 2004), coedited
by Timothy M. Smeeding and Lee Rainwater, appeared posthumously; it contains an introduction and paper cowritten by Moynihan.

I was discovering more writings and speeches by Moynihan even as I com-
pleted this manuscript. Their range and volume are extraordinary, and all I can
say with confidence about the sources I have highlighted here as well as the
hundreds, likely thousands, I consumed in researching this book is that though
I hope they are representative, they are certainly not exhaustive.

Index